MURDER *in*
VICTORIAN DAYTON

The Tragic Story of Bessie Little

SARA KAUSHAL

THE
History
PRESS

Published by The History Press
Charleston, SC
www.historypress.com

All images courtesy of Newspapers.com unless otherwise noted.

First published 2025

Manufactured in the United States

ISBN 9781467157742

Library of Congress Control Number: 2024949770

Notice: The information in this book is true and complete to the best of our knowledge. It is offered without guarantee on the part of the author or The History Press. The author and The History Press disclaim all liability in connection with the use of this book.

To Bessie
You deserved better

CONTENTS

INTRODUCTION

One of the main thoughts I had while researching and writing this story was that Bessie was wronged by so many people in her short life. She was well-liked and had many friends, but her family and her lover failed her massively. In death, she was disrespected many times again. There was one person who never knew her in life but was her champion. Chief Farrell knew something was suspicious about her death, and he didn't give up until he found the truth.

There are a few things I hope you keep in mind when reading this book:

There have been several stories written about Bessie and Albert over time. During my deep dive into research for this story, I discovered that there was way more to the case than had been written about before, which may change some things you thought you knew about Bessie and Albert.

The quotes published in newspapers were mostly just paraphrased statements presented as direct quotes. It was common to do this at the time.

Spelling was not considered an important detail in articles. A lot of names were misspelled, and you will see that in the photo captions.

There are some grisly details mentioned in this book, and I chose to leave them in to keep the full story together, the good and bad. I hope this gives a full picture of what happened.

Chapter 1

BESSIE AND ALBERT

As the warm temperature of the summer day dipped into a cool evening, Bessie hurried to eat the meat and potatoes Mrs. Freese had prepared. Bessie was running late to meet her beau, Albert. They had planned a buggy ride at six o'clock, and as she rushed out the door, it was already ten minutes past that time. Bessie hastily called out a goodbye to Mrs. Freese, who ran the boardinghouse at 208 South Jefferson Street. She headed east on Fifth Street to catch the westbound Fifth Street Car, boarded the car around six fifteen and sat directly in front of a woman she knew.

Bessie Little was a sweet and beautiful girl, well-liked by all who knew her. She was a hard worker, employed as a domestic servant from the time she was old enough to work. Bessie grew up at 1637 West Second Street, socialized in higher circles in West Dayton and regularly attended church, giving her a stellar reputation in Victorian Dayton society.

At a friend's party, she met Albert Frantz, a stenographer and general clerk at the Mathias Planing Mill. Albert lived at 1609 West Second Street, not far from Bessie's home. Albert was a few years younger than Bessie, but he charmed her instantly. She had been entertaining his company for over a year by the time she left her home and took up residence at a boardinghouse.

Albert's family were German Baptists and members of the Dunkard (also known as Dunker) Church. The term *Dunkard* originated from the practice of dunking believers three times facing forward during baptism. Albert was raised amid these surroundings, and his brother Isaac was a Dunkard preacher.

Left: Artist's depiction of Bessie Little. *Right*: Photo of Albert J. Frantz.

Albert was not considered especially handsome, even getting the moniker "dog face" from many who knew him. He was described as cunning and cruel and also spoiled. Albert was the youngest of five children and was doted on by not only his wealthy parents but by his older siblings, too. Despite his flaws, Albert was charismatic and able to charm anyone he encountered, including pretty Bessie Little.

It was charming Bessie that got them both into trouble. Albert devoted most of his time and attention to Bessie, and it worked like a charm. During their courtship, Bessie and Albert were caught in some compromising situations, which led to Mrs. Little delivering an ultimatum: leave Albert or leave the house. Bessie chose the latter, boarding first at the Hotel Cooper and then moving to Mrs. Freese's boardinghouse. It was around the time Bessie switched from the first boardinghouse to the next that Albert accompanied her to consult a physician, on suspicion she was pregnant. It was on the night of August 27, 1896, that Bessie left Mrs. Freese's boardinghouse to meet Albert for a drive in his buggy.

When Bessie disembarked at her destination, she got into Albert's buggy, and together the two rode into Dayton's true crime history.

From Albert's own account, the two took a scenic route around Dayton View, heading back over the new bridge spanning the Stillwater River. This was a route they'd taken before. According to Albert, they stopped on the bridge, looking for the wreckage of a boat that sank a few days prior. Minutes later, two shots would ring out, ending the life of pretty little Bessie. The horse pulling the buggy panicked, taking off from the bridge down the lane. Once Albert was able to regain control of the horse, he drove the buggy back to the bridge and stopped. A moment later, Bessie's body was shoved from the buggy over the rail and plunged into the water below.

Later that night, a visitor left the Frantz house and entered the alley behind it, carrying a large bundle in his arms.

The next day, Albert arrived at Mrs. Freese's boardinghouse to pay another week's board for Bessie. At his insistence, Mrs. Freese completed the transaction and provided Albert with a receipt. Mrs. Freese told Albert that Bessie had not returned from their date the night before and Albert denied meeting with her. Mrs. Freese told Albert that Bessie said she was meeting with him, and Albert insisted Mrs. Freese was wrong, that Bessie never said that and they didn't meet. He told her Bessie would return soon enough. He said Bessie must have gone home.

That evening, drama ensued at the Frantz house when the barn went up in flames. The buggy, the clothing Albert wore on the night of August 27 and his horse were locked inside.

Chapter 2

THE BODY

Discovery of the Body

The afternoon of September 2, 1896, was hot, and Eddie L. Harper was looking to cool off with a dip in the Miami River, just outside Phillip's Boat House. Harper hadn't been in the water for more than twenty minutes before he noticed a woman's shoe floating in the water nearby. Initially, the shoe appeared to be attached to a stick, but on closer inspection, Harper realized the shoe was on a foot, attached to a bloated corpse just below the surface of the water. Harper immediately notified the proprietor of the Boat House, who called the police. Her body was pulled to shore by her dress. Police Chief Farrell arrived with a patrol wagon, Officers Mikesell and Hauser, Dr. Fred Weaver and several newspaper reporters. The patrol wagon provided stretchers, which were carried into the water to retrieve the body, which was then placed in the patrol wagon.

First Exam

Once the body arrived at O.P. Boyer's undertaking establishment on West Third Street, Dr. Weaver performed an external exam, noting no bruises or wounds.

The body was in bad condition, swollen to the point it was no longer recognizable. The dress was bursting at the seams from the swelling of the

'E.L HARPER FINDING THE BODY IN THE MIAMI RIVER

Bessie's body was dragged to shore to be taken to the coroner's office.

body. The dress was one piece, a brownish color, tangled at the neck in such a way that it had to be cut from the body. The victim wore no underskirt but had on undergarments, a corset, black stockings and button shoes. Her shoes appeared to be new, branded Diers & Tanner on the inside. Her hair was messy from the time spent in the water but had originally been braided and pinned close to the head with rubber hairpins. A crawfish was spotted in her hair, and Officer Mikesell attempted to remove it, only to notice hair and scalp coming off along with its pincers. The skin of the hands and feet fell off.

Although they could tell the body was that of a young woman in her twenties, they could not make an identification. They could discern she had a low forehead and a turned-up nose. Her tongue protruded through her clenched teeth, one of which had a gold filling. Her eyes were small and blue, and her hair was dark brown. She had small hands and feet; her shoes were a size 4. The stench coming from her body was strong, driving most from the room within minutes

Reacting to the odor, undertaker Boyer declared the body could not remain in his office any longer. Since coroner Lee Corbin was out in the country, Boyer waited until he returned later that day to review the remains.

After doing so, he gave the order for burial. The body was laid on a bed of sawdust in a zinc-lined pine box, painted a drab color on the outside and given six handles for carrying. This coffin was specially made for the body, as the remains would not fit in a standard-size coffin. It was nailed up and placed inside the undertaker's carriage for transport to burial the next day, September 3.

Due to the sensational nature of the discovery, police consulted with Dr. Corbin, Dr. Bonner and Dr. Weaver, and they determined an autopsy should be performed. Undertaker Boyer would not allow the autopsy to take place at his office due to the smell, so the body was taken to Woodland Cemetery to be examined under a tent in the open air.

Second Exam

The autopsy was performed by Dr. Fred Weaver and his father, Dr. J.M. Weaver, and it was determined that although the body was in a bad state of decomposition, there was no foul play. The internal organs were examined, and the womb was found to be empty. Bessie was not pregnant, nor had she been recently. There were no signs of any operation to end a pregnancy, and one had not been performed for at least a month prior to her death. No broken bones were discovered, and the organs were decomposed but undamaged. The clothing was kept as evidence, and the cause of death was determined to be suicide by drowning. The body was buried for the first time in a potter's field, a cemetery for unclaimed or unidentified bodies.

Although the cause of death was determined to be suicide or accidental drowning, Chief Farrell had suspicions about the young woman's death. He had recently heard a rumor of two men consulting Judge Kreitzer and asking what degree of responsibility might be held against them if they knew the details of a young woman's death. When questioned, Judge Kreitzer would not divulge the names of the men, nor would he share what advice he gave them due to professional secrecy. The rumors were enough for Chief Farrell to suspect the dead woman to be a victim of foul play, not an accident or suicide.

CHIEF FARRELL.

Thomas J. Farrell, chief of police.

The next day, Mrs. Amanda Bell, bookkeeper at the Hotel Cooper, walked into the police station to report a friend of hers missing and to see if the body found was hers. Chief Farrell took her to Woodland Cemetery, where the body was exhumed for identification. Although it was not the friend Mrs. Bell had in mind, she did recognize the woman as Bessie Little, who had boarded at the Hotel Cooper for several weeks over the summer.

IDENTIFICATION

To verify that the body found was Bessie Little's, Dr. L.E. Custer, her dentist, was called in to identify her by her teeth. Dr. Custer kept meticulous notes of all the work he had done on each patient, and through his notes, he was able to identify Bessie. Over the course of time, as his patient, she'd had fifteen fillings, three of which were in the same tooth. All these records matched with the corpse. After Dr. Custer identified Bessie, her foster parents, Peter and Elizabeth Little, were called in to identify her. Despite identifying her as their daughter, they refused to take responsibility for her reburial, with Mrs. Little coldly stating that Bessie was already dead to her long ago.

DAYTON POLICE STATION.

Albert was housed at the Dayton Police Station until he was transferred to the jail.

The body identified, Chief Farrell went to work retracing her steps in the days prior to her death. Realizing Albert was the last to see her, Chief Farrell arrested him. Initially, Chief Farrell arrested Albert on the charge of murder, but he also had suspicion of another crime: illegal operation. Hearing rumors that Bessie may have been pregnant, Chief Farrell suspected Albert had arranged for an operation to be performed on her and she may have passed away as a result. Farrell suspected he could have thrown Bessie over the side of the bridge to hide the crime. There was no evidence of this, but the suspicion was enough to hold Albert while he investigated.

Albert was barely in handcuffs when Chief Farrell learned of three boys who had discovered tortoiseshell hair combs near a pool of blood on the bridge the day after

Bessie's death. Frank Ross, William Sigler and Frank Shipley had been fishing and were walking home over the bridge when they found the combs. The combs were tortoiseshell, with brilliants adorning the top edges. They had been purchased at a store called Newsalt's and were identified by Mr. Newsalt himself. Mrs. Bell of the Hotel Cooper verified she had seen Bessie wearing the side combs, and Mrs. Freese also verified the combs belonged to Bessie and confirmed Albert had given them to her. The box in which the side combs came was found in Bessie's room at the boardinghouse.

When Chief Farrell questioned Albert, he denied seeing her the night of her death. Although Albert admitted he was engaged to Bessie and said they had an intimate relationship, he denied knowledge of her disappearance. When Bessie left her

HOUSE OF MRS. DREESE,
To Which Frantz Took Bessie Little After She Left Her Home.

Mrs. Freese's boardinghouse, located on South Jefferson Street.

parents' home, Albert paid her board at the Hotel Cooper, then again at Mrs. Freese's boardinghouse.

CORONER'S INQUEST

A coroner's inquest is conducted by the coroner or deputy coroner as an inquiry into the cause of a person's death. The inquest is conducted with a smaller jury of citizens from the county and is done when the coroner is not satisfied with the cause of a person's death. This can often be the first step in a murder investigation.

On September 4, coroner Corbin, acting with Chief Farrell, decided to open a coroner's inquest to begin the official investigation into the case. County prosecuting attorney Kumler was present to assist Coroner Corbin. During this time:

Dr. Levitt Custer confirmed he had identified Bessie by her dental records.

Mrs. Bell testified that Bessie first came to the Hotel Cooper on July 25 and stayed until August 20. During this time, the ladies had become well

CORONER CORBIN.
[Who Is Investigating the Mysterious Case.]

Coroner Corbin opened the inquest investigating Bessie's death.

acquainted, and Bessie told Mrs. Bell of her troubles with Albert. Bessie told Mrs. Bell she was forced to leave home because she would not cut ties with Albert when her mother told her to do so. She also told Mrs. Bell that, several times, she'd had thoughts of suicide and that Albert promised to marry her but could not because of objections from his father. Mrs. Bell also identified the brown dress as clothing Bessie wore during her stay at the Hotel Cooper.

Mrs. Freese said Bessie came to her boardinghouse on August 20 and stayed until August 27, the night of her death. Bessie told Mrs. Freese she had thoughts of drowning herself. Mrs. Freese said she had a conversation with Albert the day after Bessie disappeared and he paid a week's board in advance. Mrs. Freese didn't want to take it until she knew Bessie would return, but Albert insisted.

Judge Kreitzer went on the stand but refused to give the names of the two men who went to him for advice regarding responsibility for withholding information about a drowned woman. Although he admitted to advising the two men, Judge Kreitzer refused to reveal their identities, claiming them both to be his clients. He said despite the fact that he advised them on the disposition of a woman's body, he had no way of knowing it was related to this case. It was during this testimony that he revealed he was also Albert's attorney.

Chief Farrell recounted the case from the beginning from his point of view, detailing the events and the discovery of evidence.

Dr. Fred Weaver and Dr. J.M. Weaver recounted the autopsy and exam performed on the corpse.

Coroner Corbin intended to question Albert on the matter, but Judge Kreitzer objected and would not allow Albert to speak. Albert said he wished he could unburden his mind and share what he knew, but he could not do so at the time.

Mr. and Mrs. Little testified to their relationship with Bessie, whom they brought home at a young age. They went to the Foundlings Home in Miami County and met a toddler named Doty, believed to be around two years old. The child's birth mother brought her to the home because she was too indisposed to care for her. The child's birth father was unknown. The little girl immediately went to Mrs. Little and held her arms out to be picked up. The childless couple decided right then to take her home. They never followed through with the legal adoption, but they raised her as their own daughter and didn't tell her otherwise. Bessie later learned the truth from friends at school and subsequently lost interest in learning and quit school early.

Mr. and Mrs. Little never suspected anything scandalous about Bessie and Albert's relationship until they were informed by the neighbors. When Mr. Little and a neighbor decided to intervene in the couple's meetings in the barn, Albert cried and promised to never meet with Bessie again. It wasn't long until they learned Albert was meeting Bessie late at night in the house. Mr. Little waited one night and chased Albert away. Albert left in such a hurry that he left his shoes behind. It was then that Mrs. Little told Bessie she had to drop Albert or leave home. Bessie chose to leave.

Mrs. Little testified that Bessie returned three times to retrieve clothing, and the last time she did, she told her mother she and Albert were getting married in a week. During that same visit, she also mentioned to her mother that she was afraid to go riding with Albert. She said he always carried a gun with him and she feared for her life.

Dr. O.E. Francis, a physician from the west side, told of Bessie's visits to him for treatment. Albert had taken Bessie to his office to examine her for signs of pregnancy. Dr. Francis examined her and believed her to be pregnant, prescribing a drug to treat nausea. He would not prescribe any medication to eliminate the pregnancy, although he said Albert implied he wanted it.

When Chief Farrell notified Corbin he was done sending him witnesses, he asked him to return an official verdict. At the beginning of the inquest, Coroner Corbin believed Bessie's death was a suicide. By the end, he stated the following:

> *After hearing the evidence and examining the body I do find the deceased Bessie Little came to her death by a pistol shot in the head. Testimony points so strong to Albert Frantz as being the murderer that I am justified in holding him over for examination before the higher courts.*

Judge Kreitzer requested Albert be removed to the county jail instead of the Central Police Station and was granted the request. In jail, Albert had the same privileges as the other prisoners, such as wholesome meals and good beds, and he was not confined to a cell. All these accommodations were not available at the Central Police Station, where Albert spent a night and a day. Albert's mood was better as a result. He dressed well and kept his appearance neat and clean, which made him look less "criminal."

The jail in which Frantz was confined.

A reporter called to the jail the next day asking to speak to Albert for an interview. Albert refused, acting on the advice of his attorney. During his stay in jail, Albert would speak only to his attorneys and family members. If any visitor called on him in jail, he would retreat to the farthest corner of his cell once he realized they were there for curiosity's sake.

Prosecutor Kumler and ex-prosecutor Patterson began getting the case in order to take it in front of the grand jury.

Third Exam of the Body

To obtain new information, Chief Farrell ordered Bessie's body to be exhumed for the second time and examined for the third. Dr. Fred Weaver, Dr. J.M. Weaver and Dr. C.N. Chrisman performed this exam. This time, they examined her head and, hidden inside the right ear, found a bullet wound. The water had washed away the blood, and the location had been obscured. The skull was fractured just above the right ear. They were able to determine the shooter was sitting on her right side, and a large bruise led them to believe he likely struck her with a rock or the butt of the gun, knocking her unconscious to facilitate her shooting. Splintered pieces of bullet were found inside the skull and dispersed throughout the brain. A larger chunk of lead had passed through the head and lodged itself next to the left ear. For evidence, the surgeons removed the head and placed it in a large glass jar containing alcohol. The jar and its contents then became the possession of the police department. Bessie's body was then buried for the third time.

During this time, hundreds of people called Dr. Fred Weaver's office, asking to see the jar containing Bessie's head. All these callers were denied their request and received a scathing lecture.

Chief Farrell, Dr. J. Weaver, Dr. Fred Weaver and Dr. Chrisman had also gone to the bridge where Bessie met her death to look for more evidence. Chief Farrell found a large pool of blood with wagon wheel marks leading from it in a long line, indicating the wheel had run through the pool of blood. He found blood marks on the railing, showing where Bessie's body would have been pushed over the side. Splinters of wood from the bridge floor were taken by Dr. Fred Weaver for chemical analysis. Chief Farrell and Dr. Fred Weaver also examined the dress worn by Bessie when she was found. Despite the time spent in the water, bloodstains were still evident on the dress. Through chemical and microscopical tests, Dr.

Above: Bessie's head was removed for use as evidence in the trial.

Opposite: Scenes from the Bessie Little murder. *Top right*: One of the magnets used to drag the riverbed for the pistol. *Lower left*: The side combs found on the bridge. *Center left*: "Cross shows where blood spots were found."

CROSS SHOWS WHERE BLOOD SPOTS WERE FOUND.

ONE OF THE MAGNETS.

THE SIDE-COMBS FOUND BY CHIEF FARRELL.

SWIMMING FLOAT AT PHILLIPS' BATH HOUSE WHERE BODY WAS FOUND.

Scenes in the Bessie Little Murder Mystery.

Chrisman and Dr. Fred Weaver were able to prove the bloodstains on all the evidence were human blood. Strands of human hair found matted in clots of blood on the bridge railing were matched to the hair from Bessie's corpse.

Chapter 3

INVESTIGATING ALBERT

Chief Farrell was suspicious of the timing of the blaze at the Frantz home and went to work investigating the remnants of the fire. Albert was seen running about during the fire wearing only shirtsleeves (no jacket, unusual during that time), leading Farrell to believe Albert had removed his jacket and thrown it into the buggy before setting the fire himself. The buggy was heavily burned but not completely consumed. Farrell was able to tear some strips from a discolored section of the buggy seat. He submitted them to the chemist for testing. He took the wagon wheel to the bridge and lined it up with the wheel track in the bloodstain on the bridge floor. It was a perfect match.

Albert behaved suspiciously during the events of the fire as well. Witnesses reported that a part of the boardwalk leading from the barn to the house had caught fire, causing a neighbor to remove boards to prevent the fire from spreading. Albert, who had been watching the blaze indifferently, sprang into action, grabbing the boards and putting them back in place. Onlookers were confused by this action, as it should have had no benefit to Albert at the time—unless he was hiding something under those boards.

Albert also intervened when a firefighter attempted to go into the barn to rescue the horse, saying, "I will let no man risk his life for that horse."

Albert was seen in a light-colored suit on the night of Bessie's murder. The next day, at work, he was seen wearing a dark-colored suit. This was so unusual for him that many employees noticed, prompting one of his companions to say, "Dog Face has got on a dark suit today."

THE FRANTZ RESIDENCE,
Showing the Burned Barn in the Rear.

During Farrell's search of the burned barn, he found a small scrap of cloth that appeared to be from the suit. It looked to have blood spots on it and was also submitted for testing. It is believed, however, that the light suit was in the suspicious bundle seen carried out of the Frantz house the night Bessie was murdered.

A constable by the name of Wallace reported to Chief Farrell regarding two men seen leaving the Frantz house the Sunday after the murder. It was around midnight, and the men were behaving suspiciously, catching Constable Wallace's attention. One man carried a large bundle in his arms while the other trailed behind, glancing around furtively as if guilty of wrongdoing.

Later, one of the men called on Chief Farrell to talk about the incident. He was a relative of Albert's, and his identity was not released to the public. When asked by Farrell what was in the bundle and what he did with it, the relative balked and refused to answer any more questions.

Bessie's remaining effects were taken from Mrs. Freese's boardinghouse and examined. A letter dated August 11 that Bessie wrote to Jacob Frantz, Albert's father, was among those items. In this letter, Bessie told Albert's father of her "ruin," caused by Albert, and begged the older Frantz to allow his son to marry her before it was too late. She said if nothing was done, she'd be forced to return home and share the details with her parents. Bessie also told the elder Frantz that Albert had taken her to a West Side physician in an attempt to get her medicine to "remedy" her situation. Bessie also wrote that she had previous trouble of the same type with Albert, but the first time it was resolved with medicine, the effects of which nearly killed her.

When confronted about this letter, Albert admitted Bessie's claims were true but stated he was unable to marry Bessie at the time because he was not yet the age of majority (twenty-one for men, eighteen for women). He claimed he was waiting to receive his inheritance from his mother on his birthday in November.

Chief Farrell released a statement to the public about the developing case:

That man murdered Bessie sure as fate, and I'll fasten the crime on him if the heavens fall. She left Mrs. Freese's boarding house the evening she was murdered at 6:10, saying she should have been off long ago. This indicates that she had an appointment undoubtedly with her lover. He made that appointment for the purpose of disposing of her, of murdering her. He chose the bridge near the Athletic Park, because he knew that the road was seldom traveled, and scarcely after dark. He murdered that girl on the bridge, in the buggy, her blood soaking the buggy cushions and running down on the wheel, which left its bloody trace on the bridge. After throwing her body over the bridge, Frantz drove to his home, and after putting his horse and buggy in the stable, he fired it, sacrificed his horse and buggy, and all to destroy all evidences of his crime. The daily papers published an account of the fire and of the burning up of the horse and buggy. The firemen could not even get into the stable when they reached it. It was locked up all around, by this man Frantz to keep them out until the buggy was burned up. The body of the girl probably laid in the water just where Frantz threw it, and then bloated and floated down the Stillwater to the Miami River, and then to the point where it was found.

JAILER JOHN WOODS.

WOMAN'S DEP'T WHERE FRANTZ IS CONFINED.

THE ACCUSED MURDERER IN HIS CELL.

Over suicide concerns, Albert was moved to the women's department of the jail.

In an attempt to get more information, Chief Farrell sent over to the jail for Albert, who was in the charge of Detective Perry. As Perry walked Albert from the jail, he attempted to draw him into conversation, but all Albert would say was, "It is a very fine day."

Walking into the office, Albert nervously looked around. He had spent a restless night on the hard couch in his cell, tossing and turning. The strain was apparent in his countenance. A slight beard was coming in, adding to the overall haggard appearance of the prisoner. Albert appeared to have aged years in the short time he had spent in jail so far.

The inmates in the jail were allowed razors on certain days of the week to take care of their facial hair, but jailer Wood would not allow Albert to have one, over concerns he might make an attempt on his life. Albert had been confined to the women's department of the jail and given roommates, Bert Rawlins and George Snyder, both sixteen and charged with horse theft. They were tasked with keeping his spirits up and helping keep watch over him. Wood had lost a few prisoners before to suicide and did not want to risk another occurrence.

Under questioning, Albert told Chief Farrell that Bessie had shot herself twice, confirming Farrell's theory that there were two bullets. Albert continued to explain that in a panic, he dumped her body into the river. He then threw the gun into the water after her. Albert made this confession in front of a *Dayton Herald* newspaper reporter, along with reporters from other newspapers. Initially, Albert refused to answer any questions Farrell asked in front of anyone else, but when he realized Farrell would not relent, he gave this partial confession:

> *On Thursday, August 27, I met Bessie by appointment on the boulevard. It was about 6. We drove around Dayton View, and on our way back took the old road to the new bridge over Stillwater River. When we got there she pulled out a revolver and before I knew what she was going to do, shot herself. I was so frightened that I took the body and dropped it over the railing into the water. Then I tossed the revolver over too.*

Albert denied ever having owned a revolver, and when Farrell asked him why he called on Bessie's boardinghouse when he knew she was dead, Albert claimed it was because he was frightened.

On receiving this partial confession, Chief Farrell read Albert his arrest warrant, stating as follows:

> *The State of Ohio, Montgomery County, City of Dayton, ss:*
> *To the Chief of Police of said City, Greeting:*
> *Whereas, Complaint has been made before me, C.J. Mattern, Clerk of the Police Court of the City of Dayton, in the State and County aforesaid, on*

the oath of *T.J. Farrell, that Albert J. Frantz, on or about the 27th day of August, A.D., 1896, at the county of Montgomery, did as aforesaid, in and upon one Bessie Little, then and there being, unlawfully, purposely, and of deliberate and premeditated malice, make as assault in a menacing manner, with intent her the said Bessie Little, unlawfully, purposely, and, of deliberate and premeditated malice, to kill and murder, and the said Albert J. Frantz, with a certain pistol then and there charged with gunpowder and certain leaden bullets, which said pistol he, the said Albert J. Frantz, then and there in his right hand had and held, then and there unlawfully, purposefully and of premeditated malice, did discharge and shoot off to, against and upon the said Bessie Little, with the intent aforesaid, and that the said Albert J. Frantz with the leaden bullets aforesaid, out of the pistol aforesaid by the force of the gunpowder aforesaid, by the said Albert J. Frantz then and there discharged and shot off as aforesaid, her, the said Bessie Little, in and upon the head of her the said Bessie Little, then and there unlawfully, purposefully, and of deliberate and premeditated malice, did strike, penetrate and wound, with intent aforesaid, thereby then and there given to her, the said Bessie Little, with the leaden bullets aforesaid, so as aforesaid discharged and shot out of the pistol aforesaid by the aforesaid Albert J. Frantz in and upon the head of her, the said Bessie Little, one mortal wound of the depth of three inches and of the breadth of one-quarter of an inch of which said mortal wound she, the said Bessie Little, then and there died.*

T.J. Farrell does say that the said Albert J. Frantz, her, the said Bessie Little, in the manner and by the means aforesaid, unlawfully, purposely and of deliberate and premeditated malice, did kill and murder. These are, therefore, to command you to take the said Albert J. Frantz, if he be found in your county, or if he shall have fled, that you pursue after the said Albert J. Frantz into any county within this State, and take and keep the said Albert J. Frantz, so that you have his body forthwith before the Judge of Police Court of said city to answer said complaint, and be further dealt with according to law.

Given under my hand and official seal the _____ day of _____, 1896.
C.J. Mattern, Clerk of the Police Court of the City of Dayton, Ohio.

Albert listened to the charges, struggling to subdue the anxiety building inside him. When Chief Farrell asked him if he understood the charges against him, he could only nod his head in affirmation.

Although Albert's public demeanor normally appeared detached, his attitude in jail was entirely different. When Albert's sister Mattie Frantz

Albert spent his time in jail reading the Bible his sister gave him.

visited him shortly after his arrest, she brought with her a Bible and told him to get all his comfort and consolation from it. From then on, he spent his time in exaggerated religious fervor, praying and singing. Every visitor was subjected to lengthy readings of passages or singing before he'd speak to them. His favorite selections were from the "Winnowed Hymns from Sacred Song." Albert was a fairly good baritone (later described as a tenor) singer with a pleasant voice.

Mattie had been involved in a scandal of her own just three years prior. A man named Jefferson Shank was convicted of killing his wife, Nannie, with rumors circulating he had done so in hopes of marrying Mattie. Shank had been renting a farm owned by Jacob Frantz in Miami County when he met Mattie. Mattie testified during Shank's trial that she and Nannie quickly became best friends, spending lots of time together. Jefferson, Nannie and Mattie socialized extensively, often attending the same parties. Shank was adamant it wasn't just Mattie and him attending parties together but that his wife and Albert had also attended most of those parties with them. He always maintained his innocence, claiming his wife was killed by burglars. He was convicted on strong circumstantial evidence and claimed his confession was fabricated by the detectives investigating the case. At the time of Albert's trial, Shank was serving a life sentence in the Ohio Penitentiary.

As Albert was being led back to the jail, he asked Chief Farrell if he could shave. Farrell gave permission for Detective Perry to send for a barber to shave Albert at the jail. When he heard this, Albert stopped in his tracks, ran his hand through his short beard and considered this option for a moment.

"Chief, I guess it is not necessary to shave me now. I do not want it." Albert responded.

"Alright, just as you like," Farrell replied.

For hours after returning to the jail, Albert was too depressed to resume his normal routine of reading passages from the Bible and singing hymns.

The Two Men

Chief Farrell learned the identities of the two men who consulted Judge Kreitzer regarding a dead woman in the river before Bessie was discovered. He agreed to keep their identities secret from the public if the two men cooperated and gave their statements. One man stated he had advised Albert to confess to the police, but what exactly he was to confess was not revealed by the police. The other man said he knew of the murder before finding the body. Both men were very agitated while telling their stories, one seeking solace in the Bible during his telling. Neither man had any part in the murder, nor were they in any way to be criminally implicated. During the interviews, Judge Kreitzer, prosecutor Kumler and ex-prosecutor Patterson were present. A stenographer was there to record their statements and copies would be given to both the prosecution and the defense.

Where Was the Crime Scene?

Chief Farrell had yet to determine where exactly Bessie was shot. Many believed Bessie was murdered on the bridge and immediately dumped over the side, but there was no evidence of a scuffle on the bridge. Several pools and spots of blood were found on the bridge, and a wheel mark in one of those blood pools led many to believe the bridge was the crime scene. Based on the wheel marks, the body may have hung from the buggy over the wheel, the blood running down the wheel onto the ground.

The fact that Bessie was thrown over the bridge indicated she was attacked either on or near the bridge. The bridge lay at the foot of a bluff and in the shadow of forest trees, a secluded area. A densely wooded ravine located roughly four hundred feet westward along the roadway from the bridge showed signs of a scuffle. Blood spots and a blood trail led police to believe it could have been the spot where Albert attacked Bessie.

Placing the Time of the Murder

The woman who had seen Bessie get on the streetcar and sit in front of her cooperated with Chief Farrell, in exchange for secrecy regarding her identity. She recalled distinctly seeing Bessie at about 6:15 or 6:20 p.m. on August 27, a fact she remembered so well because she was heading home after attending the funeral of a friend. She did not pay much attention to Bessie at the time, as her attention was caught by a group of lady cyclists riding by the car. She noticed Bessie stayed on the car for two or three stops before getting off. She couldn't say for sure, but she thought Bessie disembarked the car on the boulevard.

Witnesses who claimed to hear a woman screaming and shots agreed on the sounds they heard but disagreed on the time. Reverend A.F. Brandenburg and his family were traveling home from a family reunion in Vandalia near the bridge when they heard what they thought were shots and the cries of a woman in distress. After that, all was silent. The sounds and subsequent silence were the topic of discussion for the rest of the drive home but forgotten until news of the murder reached the papers. They fixed the time at 7:30 p.m.

Albert was seen returning to his house around 7:30 p.m., which neighbors remarked was earlier than usual for him. Chief Farrell believed Albert could have made a big show of coming home at that time to establish an alibi. Later that evening, he quietly hitched up his horse and left the house, with the plan to murder Bessie.

Three witnesses living near the bridge heard two gunshots and the sound of a woman screaming around 11:00 p.m. on August 27. Mrs. Herby, who lived a furlong (one-eighth of a mile) from the bridge, heard the sounds of two shots and a woman screaming on the night of August 27, along with two other witnesses.

A group of street sweepers noticed Albert out around 11:00 p.m., one remarking to another, "Dog Face is out rather late tonight."

Farrell had reason to believe the eyewitness accounts placing Albert on the boulevard. The witnesses were able to positively identify not only Albert but also his horse and buggy. Albert drove a phaeton buggy pulled by a bay horse. Bay is a hair coat color characterized by reddish-brown body color with black points (mane, tail, ears and lower legs). The horse was large, too big for the buggy it pulled. The buggy itself was a sporty open carriage that had been popular in the late 1700s and early 1800s but was considered old-fashioned by the 1890s. The combination of a too-large horse and an old-fashioned buggy made a memorable sight.

During the night in question, Albert claimed to have been out collecting debts for the planing mill. A man named Ambrose remembered Albert calling on him to collect a debt around that time in August but could not recall the exact date. He noted that Albert was in a rather excited state and seemed to be in a hurry to collect.

Chapter 4

THE SEARCH FOR THE REVOLVER

Chief Farrell went to work to search the riverbed below the bridge. A diver by the name Phillips, son of the boathouse proprietor, was secured to search for the revolver. He made several trips to the bottom of the river but was unable to find it.

After this attempt failed, Farrell rigged up a battery made of a large magnet shaped like a horseshoe, six inches long and three inches wide, weighing about three pounds. The magnet was expected to have a draw of about six inches, attracting any steel item up to one pound. To ensure the magnet worked, Farrell experimented at the police station using a large bucket of water and a revolver. Once he confirmed the magnet would work and the water would not provide any resistance to the magnet attracting steel, he ordered eleven more to be made. He then had them heavily charged at the electric light works in Dayton View.

Chief Farrell then met with Boatman Ritter to begin the search. The magnets were lowered with ropes from two boats to the bottom of the river, the boats moving slowly over the water. Chief Farrell and Sergeant Kelly supervised the search, working all night.

The magnets did not result in finding the revolver, but the searchers did not finish empty-handed. A sewing machine shuttle, an iron pipe and several pieces of iron and steel were brought to the surface using the magnets. At one point, one magnet caught a heavy object, but as the magnet was drawn to the surface, the object clinging to it fell. The magnet was thrown back

Dredging the river with magnets, searching for Frantz's revolver.

a second time and again attracted the object. Again the object fell before coming to the surface. For the third time, the object was drawn to the surface—and this time, secured. Finally, the object breached the surface of the water, and excitedly, the men hurried to see what they found, sure they had finally found the revolver. It was an iron wrench.

They hadn't found the revolver yet, but this latest find motivated them to continue the search. Mr. J.C. Norris of 116 South Williams Street called on Chief Farrell to loan him a powerful magnet to use in the search. Mr. Norris said he used this magnet to lift axes from the northern reservoirs where he was employed. It would easily pick up a revolver. Chief Farrell was eager to continue the search but had made arrangements with a diver named Ben Graham from Cincinnati if the magnets didn't work.

Ben Graham was a well-known diver in Cincinnati, one of the best. His father was a famous diver, and Ben followed in his footsteps, making a great reputation for himself. Graham had experience exploring the Ohio River to help in cases of wrecked boats.

SEARCHING FOR THE REVOLVER.

Chief Farrell, boatman Ritter and Sergeant Kelly lowered magnets attached to ropes into the water.

When another sun set with no results from the magnet search, Chief Farrell sent a telegram to diver Graham, who was ready to board the train to Dayton as soon as he received notice. Graham agreed to work for costs covered, saying, "If I can help justice in a case of this kind, I will gladly."

Once he arrived in Dayton, diver Graham visited the river with Chief Farrell, and the two made arrangements for him to start work immediately. After examining the location and the water, Graham assured Farrell that if the revolver was in the water, he would find it.

A local man named Ferdinand Glass was rowing about the search area holding a stick over the water. When asked, he explained he was using a divining rod, also known as a dip needle, in attempts to help find the revolver. The rod was made from the Y-shaped sprig of a tree, containing a small bottle of quicksilver fastened to a slit on the joined end. The rod is held in each hand at the Y, Glass explained, and if it dips down toward the water, there is surely metal below. Personal magnetism plays a large part in the matter, he explained, and he had found hidden objects on land with the

Left: Diver Ben Graham. *Right*: Graham in his diving apparatus lowering himself into the water.

rod before. Several skeptics were convinced of the rod's validity when Glass found a dollar they had hidden in the bank as a test.

On the morning of Graham's first descent, a detail of police (Police Captain Allaback, Detective Sergeant Keller, Detective Perry, Detective Clayton and Officer O'Brian) was present at the bridge ready to hold back the large crowd forming and render assistance to the dive. Hundreds of spectators lined the riverbank, eager to get a look at the equipment.

Officers removed the diving apparatus from the patrol wagon. Two men had to operate the air pump, which forced air through a long rubber hose into the diver's suit. The suit, which was a large canvas sack, was weighted with lead. The air from the pump was forced through the rubber tube into the headpiece, which was a round metal air boiler with glass bullseye windows and an air exit. The air was forced through the headpiece and out the air exit, bubbling to the surface of the water.

The air pump was set up on the bridge and the rubber tube dropped over the side of the bridge in the spot where Albert claimed to have thrown Bessie and the revolver into the river. The diving suit shoes had lead soles to weigh Graham down in the water, allowing him to stay at the bottom of the river.

Graham and several boatmen rowed out to the spot in the water, believing the revolver was at the location. They fastened a rope to the diving suit, and Graham made his first descent into the water. The depth of the water at that point was roughly twelve to fifteen feet. Graham made several descents that morning, each lasting fifteen to twenty minutes. Around 11:00 a.m., he finally resurfaced with a large metal object, glinting in the sun. Spectators stirred, thinking he had finally found the revolver, but alas, it was just a bicycle wrench. It appeared to have been thrown in the river recently, having gathered no rust.

Diver Graham was losing hope. It had been several days since he started the search, and none of the descents had resulted in surfacing anything besides pieces of trash and metal tools. Farrell decided to try one more method before giving up. He thought maybe the revolver had sunk deeper into the soft mud at the bottom of the riverbed, which is why it hadn't been unearthed yet. Prongs were dropped into the water and allowed to sink into the mud. Once deep enough, they were dragged along the bottom, hoping to loosen anything that could have been caught in the mud.

Graham continued the search on the riverbed, digging into the soft earth with his hands. He dug so deep he reached the nests of turtles and crawfish. The crawfish attacked his fingers, prompting Graham to surface and put on his rubber mittens, covered in canvas. At the end of the day, Graham climbed back into the barge and told Chief Farrell that the gun was definitely not in the river near the upper side of the bridge. Farrell agreed and said the next day, they would work on the lower side.

Another diver, A.E. Pate, came from Toledo to aid in the search for the revolver. Pate was a champion diver and swimmer, and he was set to work the edges of the river while Graham worked the depths. Pate dove in only a pair of swimming trunks and made several attempts, working his way through the mud with his bare hands. Pate attracted a lot of attention with one dive in particular, searching the mud from one shore nearly to the other side, digging through the mud at the bottom. Pate was in agreement with Farrell and Graham: the pistol was not in the water on the upper side of the bridge.

The crowd continued to grow larger as the search progressed. The spectators, numbering into the hundreds, lined the riverbanks on both sides on foot, in carriages and on bicycles. They lined up above and below the bridge, coming on boats on the

A. E. PATE,
Champion swimmer of the Northwest, now engaged in the search for Frantz's pistol.

White Line. There were dozens of bicycles stacked against the bridge, fifteen to twenty carriages along the banks and about a dozen boats on the water, all filled with curious onlookers. Among the spectators were prosecutor Kumler, ex-prosecutor Patterson and coroner Corbin, all wanting to be informed of any developments. Luckily, Farrell had collected all his evidence from the bridge, because spectators were taking small pieces of the bridge for macabre souvenirs.

It was during this time that Farrell received another tip. A man had come forward but would only agree to share his story if his identity was kept absolutely confidential. Once he was assured by Farrell, he recounted his tale.

Just after Bessie's disappearance, he was walking near the bridge when he encountered a man wearing a light suit who seemed to be looking for something in the weeds. The witness claimed the strange man asked him if he had seen a revolver lying along the road as he walked. The witness answered that he had not and continued on his walk. It wasn't until he heard of the case that he connected the information to it and came forward.

During these sessions, the divers were also looking for Bessie's hat, which had not turned up in the search of the barn or river.

BUYING THE GUN

During the course of his investigation, Farrell learned where Albert had gotten the gun: from a store owned by James Dodds. The clerk who had sold the gun to Albert, J.W. Poince, distinctly remembered the transaction and Albert.

The young man had entered the store, and Poince asked him what kind of weapon he wanted to purchase. Albert shrugged and said, "Just an ordinary pistol."

Poince laid out three .32-caliber revolvers on the case. Albert picked up one and asked the price, which was $3.00. Without hesitation, he said he would take it. Poince asked Albert if he was of age, and he said he was, so Poince wrapped it for him. Albert then asked for cartridges and, again, asked for the price, which was $0.75. Albert paid the $3.75 and left.

The entire interaction stood out to Poince because of Albert's peculiar behavior. Usually, customers looked at several guns before making a choice, but Albert bought the first one he touched. Poince was also struck by the young age of his customer.

FRANTZ APPEARS IN POLICE COURT.

Clockwise from top left: J.W. Poince, the salesman who sold Albert the revolver in question; Colonel Robert Nevin; Judge Kreitzer, one of Albert's attorneys; W. Van Skaik. (Van Skaik's surname was often misspelled in the newspapers.)

Poince was unable to come into the police station to identify Albert. He was injured with a bad hip and confined to his home, so Detective Perry loaded Albert into a buggy and parked him outside Poince's home. Poince looked out the window and said he thought Albert was the man to whom he had sold the gun, but he was not entirely sure. The longer he looked, the surer he became. When Albert put on his hat, Poince nodded his head and said, "He is the man."

Chief Farrell consulted with Prosecutor McCann in hopes of procuring a warrant to search the Frantz home. It was his hope to have Detectives Keller and Perry search the home from "cellar to garret" for evidence. The letter of the law was examined thoroughly, but nothing was found to allow the search. Chief Farrell sent officers to local tailors in hopes of finding the tailor who had made Albert's suit, to no avail.

Even without a search of the home, enough evidence was gathered and Albert was arraigned in police court on a charge of murder. He was accompanied by his attorneys, Judge Kreitzer, William Van Skaik and Colonel Robert Nevin. He entered a plea of not guilty and he was set to appear before the grand jury the following Tuesday, September 15. Albert was transported back to jail after the arraignment and maintained a stoic indifference throughout these events. He refused to speak except to his attorneys. Albert was held without bond.

Chapter 5

GRAND JURY

The grand jury convened on September 15, 1896, with Judge Dale presiding. The large crowd that gathered was kept outside and admittance was limited to only witnesses relevant to the case.

Presenting the case were police prosecutor McCann, county prosecutor Kumler and the Honorable J.C. Patterson. Judge Kreitzer and W.H. Van Skaik were present to represent Albert, who was brought from the jail to the station house by patrol wagon, in the charge of Officer Mikesell. Albert was smooth-shaven and pale.

The first witness called was Charles Phillips, owner of the Boat House along the Miami River where Bessie was found. Phillips was a bespectacled, white-haired, middle-aged man with a gray beard and mustache. He spoke with a mild German accent. Phillips was first asked about his Boat House, the surroundings, the river, etc. He was asked about the bridge over the Stillwater River and if there were any lights on that night, to which he answered no. Mr. Phillips testified that E.L. Harper notified his son, who in turn notified him, and he notified the police. Phillips then retrieved a pole with a hook on the end, got into his boat and towed the body to the shore to be picked up by police.

Coroner Corbin was next to be called. Corbin was out in the country when Bessie's body was discovered, so he authorized the assistant police surgeon, Dr. Fred Weaver, to perform the autopsy in his place. Corbin noted that there was a witness present during the coroner's inquest who would not testify (Albert Frantz).

Dr. Fred Weaver detailed Chief Farrell's orders to examine the body and the subsequent examinations under a tent at Woodland Cemetery. It was during the second examination that he determined Bessie's last meal to have been meat and potatoes, which were undigested. This determined the time of death: within two hours of her last meal. Bessie's internal organs were also examined at this time. Dr. Weaver accompanied Dr. Custer to the body to examine the teeth. He also performed the third examination of the body, in which the head was examined. This was not done during the prior exam. Two bullet holes were found in the skull, and from each of the holes, several fractures deviated at different angles.

Prosecutor McCann unwrapped a skull, handed it to Dr. Weaver and had him show where the bullet holes were. Dr. Weaver pointed out the bullet holes in the right side of the head and said they were undoubtedly bullet wounds and resulted in instantaneous death. Dr. Weaver described the blood spots on the bridge, taking samples of them and testing them with Dr. Chrisman.

Dr. Chrisman testified to his part in helping test the samples with Dr. Weaver.

Dr. Custer spoke of filling Bessie's teeth and identifying her through his records of those fillings.

Mrs. Elizabeth Little, Bessie's foster mother, confirmed that Albert and Bessie had been keeping company for about a year before Bessie's death. Mrs. Little had reviewed the remains at Woodland Cemetery and confirmed the body to be Bessie's. Mrs. Little put on a show of weeping bitterly in the back row of the courtroom before taking the stand. She confirmed she took Bessie in when the girl was about two years old. Bessie was a smart and pretty little girl, and the Littles raised her.

Mr. Peter Little, Bessie's foster father, told of clandestine meetings between Bessie and Albert. In one incident, Albert left in such a hurry that he left his shoes behind, which were still at the Little home.

Mrs. Bell spoke of Bessie's time staying in Hotel Cooper and of Albert paying her board. Mrs. Bell recounted a conversation with Albert in which he said he was not ready to marry Bessie, but Mrs. Bell believed Bessie was anxious to marry Albert.

Police Chief Farrell told his story, starting from finding the body and continuing through the subsequent developments. He brought with him the lead taken from Bessie's skull, which was then submitted into evidence. Farrell had arrested Albert Frantz, who denied seeing Bessie on the night of her death and claimed not to know she was dead until Chief Farrell told him so. Albert later changed his story, admitting he was with Bessie that night but that she shot herself and, in a panic, he threw her into the river.

Albert then claimed the gun was Bessie's, not his, and that he had never owned a gun.

The prosecution then called several newspaper reporters in to recount what they had heard Albert confess. After this, both prosecution and defense rested their case.

Judge Dale made a statement declaring there was no question that a crime was committed or that Albert was with Bessie the night she died. There was probable cause for thinking he murdered her, and the court felt its duty was to bind the prisoner over to the grand jury on the charge of murder in the first degree. Albert was immediately taken back to the jail. His face was pale and his demeanor dejected. The crowd gathered outside was greatly disappointed to be denied access to the events inside the courtroom. Albert's trial was set to start on December 14, 1896.

Shortly after the grand jury proceedings finished, Chief Farrell received a letter from an anonymous man. It said:

Nashville, TN Sep. 15, 1896
Captain T.J. Farrell, Dayton, Ohio
Dear Sir, I am in Nashville, and have been here since the Saturday morning after the murder of Miss Bessie Little. I was afraid to stay there because I saw a sight on that fateful night that made me almost crazy afterward, and was also afraid that I might be arrested for the crime I saw.

Will you arrest me if I come back to testify or not? I will not send my name, but you can just address your letter to the American office and make them publish it and I will watch for it and if you think I am safe I will come at once. Hoping to hear from you by return mail, I remain
Your ever true servant, AMC
Care American Newspaper, Nashville TN
P.S. My evidence would be of great help to you in the Frantz-Little case.

Chief Farrell wasn't sure if the letter was legitimate, but to be sure, he wrote back.

Dayton, Ohio, Sept. 17, 1896
AMC, Care American Office, Nashville, TN
Dear Sir: I am in receipt of your note of September 15, in which you say you are in possession of valuable information concerning the Frantz-Little murder. Permit me to say that if you have the information your letter indicates, you need not be afraid to tell me of it.

You have my positive assurance that no harm will come to you, providing, of course, that you did not have a hand in the murder, which I do not believe you had, but you are evidently afraid on account of what you saw that night. You need not be afraid to give me your name or the information that you possess, as I will neither use it or publish it until the proper time comes, and then only in the cause of justice.

Yours Truly, T.J. Farrell, Superintendent of Police

Chief Farrell wired the chief of police in Nashville, J.H. Clack, to have a detective await the arrival of AMC at the American Office Newspaper and detain him until an officer could be sent from Dayton to retrieve him. In the months before the trial, Chief Farrell heard nothing from AMC.

Chapter 6

THE TRIAL: GETTING STARTED

MONDAY, DECEMBER 14, 1896,
AND TUESDAY, DECEMBER 15, 1896

On day one of court, the spectators showed up in full force, not only filling the courtroom but also spilling into the adjacent corridors of the courthouse. The crowd of mostly ladies was eager to view or hear whatever they could of the sensational trial. By the time court started at nine o'clock, the crowd had overflowed into the street.

Jury selection filled the first few days of Albert's trial. The first venire (panel of prospective jurors) of thirty-six men was called. Both prosecution and defense made quick work of interviewing and eliminating veniremen, necessitating the use of the second venire of thirty-six by the second day.

One of the men eliminated on the first day from the first venire was John N. Morehouse, father to Johnny Morehouse, who drowned in the Miami Erie Canal in front of his home. Johnny was buried in Woodland Cemetery, and his parents had a gravestone statue created to represent the love Johnny had for his dog, prompting urban legends and ghost stories that continue to the present day. John was eliminated because he had read accounts of the case in the newspaper and had already formed an opinion of what happened in the case.

By the end of the second day, the second venire had been exhausted and there were still not enough jurors, prompting Judge Brown to order a third venire of twenty-five to be ready by the opening of court the next morning.

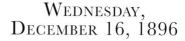

WEDNESDAY,
DECEMBER 16, 1896

By lunch on the third day, nearly one hundred men had been interviewed, and the jury of twelve had finally been selected.

The jurors selected were: Joseph Shively, farmer, Madison Township; George Davis, bricklayer, Dayton (jury foreman); Levi Mease, retired farmer, Miamisburg; Adolph Geige, molder, Dayton; Dietrich Von Engle, carpenter, Dayton; Martin Young, farmer, Van Buren Township; Captain David F. Giddinger, insurance agent, Dayton; A.H. Baker, gardener and hotelkeeper, Brookville; John Moler, farmer, Van Buren Township; Isaac Haynes, farmer, Washington Township; Elijah Coler, wagonmaker, Liberty; and Captain James W. Daugherty, druggist, Dayton.

Before proceedings began, Van Skaik asked the jury if anyone had any reason they felt unable to deliver a fair and impartial opinion in the case. Adolph Geige, a German native, said he did not understand English well and thought he should be excused. The court determined he was adequate to fill the position.

Once the jurors were secured and sworn in, they were escorted to the bridge where Bessie met her fate. The conversation among the jurors related only to the case until a lively conversation broke out between two jurors about cattle. The other ten listened intently.

The twelve men selected to decide Albert's fate.

The bridge where Bessie was killed.

Bailiff Boes took charge of the jury. With over one hundred witnesses, the case was expected to be a lengthy one.

The men were put up at the Hotel Cooper and were in the charge of bailiff Boes and his assistant, Ed Bozenhardt. They were allowed all the reading material they desired, but all newspapers were censored before being given to the men. Anything pertaining to the case, directly or indirectly, had to be removed.

After a brief recess, the opening statements began.

Prosecuting attorney Charles Kumler opened for the state and detailed the love affair between Albert and Bessie, sharing the scandal of their romance, which resulted in Bessie leaving home to be with Albert. Albert then took her to the Hotel Cooper to board but requested she be unregistered, using the excuse that he didn't want her parents to find her. Kumler recounted the incident when Albert stormed into the hotel, paid Bessie's board and declared to anyone within earshot that he was done with Bessie, as she had written a letter to his father that stirred up a lot of drama at his home. Albert left the hotel and headed to Dodd's Gun Store, buying a revolver. Then he returned to the Hotel Cooper, telling Bessie he wanted to smooth things over and he took her to Mrs. Freese's boardinghouse, where she stayed until her death.

On the night of her death, Albert took Bessie out buggy riding, then shot her twice in the head, shoving her body from the buggy into the water below. Kumler further stated that knowing Bessie was dead, Albert called at Mrs.

PROSECUTOR KUMLER.   EX-PROSECUTOR PATTERSON.

The team prosecuting Albert.

Freese's boardinghouse and insisted on paying a week's board in advance, knowing Bessie would not return but assuring Mrs. Freese that she would.

"At the time," said Kumler, "he knew that she would not be back. He knew, as he later confessed, that he had thrown her body into the river. He was weaving a web, intending to show that he was innocent but he was himself caught in the very web."

Kumler followed this statement with Albert's confession to Chief Farrell (in front of reporters) that he had thrown Bessie's body into the river and threw the revolver in after her.

As Kumler laid out the details, Albert leaned back in his chair, face pale and lips twitching in excitement. His eyes held the alarm of any man on trial for his life, whether guilty or innocent, as he heard in grim detail the murder of which he was accused.

Colonel Robert Nevin addressed the court for the defense, opening with the story of a sad courtship between two young lovers who adored each other, one ending her own life in a shocking manner. He argued that Bessie and Albert could have had a lover's pact to end their lives but that Albert backed out when it came time to fulfill his end of the deal. Nevin also harped on the fact that Bessie frequently mentioned suicide.

During Nevin's speech, Albert gasped and burst into tears, laying his head down as the tears trickled from his cheeks into small pools on the table. As if bolstered by Albert's behavior, Nevin argued that Albert was not only innocent of the crime but that he was also insane, a condition inherited from his mother's side of the family, the Studebakers.

The first witness to be called was Charles Phillips, proprietor of the Boat House along the Miami River where Bessie's body was discovered. Phillips said a young man bathing at his Boat House, E.L. Harper, found the body on September 2. The police were summoned and the body was removed.

Dr. Fred Weaver was called to give a few details while the court waited for a few more witnesses to arrive. Dr. Weaver oversaw the removal of Bessie's body from the river to the undertaker's office at around 4:30 p.m. on September 2. He saw Bessie's body at Woodland Cemetery the next morning, in the southeast corner of the potter's field. He was able to describe the clothing she wore.

Peter Little was next to take the stand. He told the story of fostering Bessie from the Miami County Infirmary when she was a small child. He hadn't seen Bessie since July, about a month before her death. He and his wife identified the body the day it was found; they saw it at the cemetery.

Elizabeth Little said she'd known Bessie since she was a toddler. Bessie had lived with the Littles nearly all her life. She left their home in July, and Elizabeth Little saw her about two weeks after that. Mrs. Little and her husband identified Bessie in Woodland Cemetery by her eyes, teeth and forehead.

Dr. Levitt E. Custer identified Bessie by her dental work. Dr. Custer had kept meticulous records of all the work he had done on Bessie since her first visit on October 7, 1892. His records were exhaustive and described every detail of work done to each tooth at every visit. Dr. Levitt examined the teeth of the corpse and was satisfied they matched those of Bessie Little.

James Stevens, assistant to undertaker Boyer, detailed taking the body to the undertaker's office and its removal to the cemetery the next morning. He said the body was placed in a zinc-lined box and covered in sawdust. Another assistant, Allen Wolf, gave the same testimony.

John Meixell, in charge of the patrol wagon, described the removal of the body from the river to the undertaker's office. Bessie's clothing was taken to the patrol house the next day.

Mrs. Minnie Freese was the proprietress of the boardinghouse where Bessie spent her last days. Bessie became her boarder on August 20, stayed for a week and left for the last time on August 27 around 6:10 p.m. She described the outfit Bessie was wearing when she left that day and was sure she would recognize it again. Police officer Mikesell brought in the clothing and held it up for the court. The sight of the clothes Bessie was wearing when she met her death was startling, and many spectators shuddered at the sight.

Court was adjourned for the day until nine o'clock the next morning.

George Mannix, an attorney staying at the Hotel Cooper at the same time as Bessie, was interviewed by the *Cincinnati Enquirer*. He told the reporter what he intended to say in court:

> *There are a few things in connection with this case that I may divulge as soon as I am placed on the stand.*
>
> *While Bessie was here, her room was next to mine, with only a thin board partition between us. She occupied room 83. Mine was 82, while Miss Bell, the hotel cashier, occupied room 84. Bessie was between us. I had understood that Bessie had a lover who was supporting her, but so far as I know, that lover, whom I afterward knew as Albert J Frantz, never called at the young lady's room.*
>
> *She was a very pretty girl, but morbid. She told me one day in the hotel corridor that she intended marrying Frantz. Miss Bell was also in the secret. Often was I kept awake at night by the unhappy girl's sobs and prayers in the next room. It was no unusual thing for her to be praying loudly at 3 and 4 o'clock in the morning. One day I was passing out of the hotel and saw Frantz leaning over the hotel desk talking to Miss Bell. I heard him say, "Yes, I will marry her, but I'll be — if I will be forced."*
>
> *August 13, unlucky day, I heard Miss Bell asking somebody at the telephone if Frantz has bought a revolver at this place that day, but don't know what answer she received. Kissinger, it seems, saw Frantz making the purchase, but got the name of the store wrong, and told Miss Bell. The latter was in sympathy with the unhappy girl, and told her what she had heard or at least said she intended to do so. Of course, at the time I knew there was trouble between the girl and Frantz, but supposing it to be only a lover's quarrel, paid little attention to it. She was a charming girl, was Bessie, refined and of sweet disposition.*

Chapter 7

THE TRIAL: HEAD CASES

Thursday, December 17, 1896

After eating a hearty breakfast, Albert was escorted into court at 8:43 a.m. He was well dressed and clean-shaven, but it was abundantly clear he hadn't slept much the previous night.

Women had been dominating the crowd of spectators, some even filling the windows of a nearby building in hopes of seeing Albert as he walked between the courtroom and the jail. Albert remained mostly somber but sometimes would cast a flirtatious glance or smile their way. The gestures had their desired effect, as the women continued to fill the windows.

Walking into the courtroom, Albert kept silent until he saw the jury. He then said, "That jury is a pretty good set of fellows." A number of his relatives filled the stands behind him, and he shook hands with and greeted them. Albert remained composed until he saw his father hobbling into court using a crutch. At the sight of his feeble father, he burst into tears. Jacob Frantz took a seat on the bench behind his son and whispered words of comfort and encouragement.

Many members of the Frantz family were Dunkards, which drew a large crowd of the Dunkard community to the trial. Dunkard bonnets were dispersed throughout the crowd, and it was rumored that two of the jurors were also members. Although Albert himself was a member of the Christian Church, his indirect affiliation drew their deep interest in the case.

The trial attracted a larger crowd from Montgomery County than anyone had seen before. The seating was filled well beyond capacity very early into the morning, and by the time Colonel Nevin had finished his statement for the defense, there was no longer room to stand in the courtroom. People were seated on the backs of chairs, in the windows and on any other flat surface they could find. It was almost impossible to walk through the crowd, the people were so tightly packed.

John Hauser, driver of the patrol wagon, was first to take the stand. Hauser described taking Bessie's body from the river to the undertaker's office.

J.C. Klein, superintendent of Woodland Cemetery, testified that the body of a woman was buried in the potter's field and disinterred the next day. Then the head was removed and taken for evidence and the body reburied.

Police surgeon Dr. Fred Weaver was next to take the stand. The first autopsy, Dr. Weaver explained, was held to examine the internal organs and the content of the stomach. He did not examine the head during the first autopsy because it was assumed Bessie had drowned. His exam showed she had a dinner of meat and potatoes, which was still undigested. This placed the time of her death within two hours of her meal. He went back later the same day to collect her clothing. Dr. Weaver identified the mud-stained brown dress and the hair that had been stripped from Bessie's head from decomposition.

Patrol wagon driver John Meixell and police secretary Frank Withoft entered the courtroom carrying a large pine box and set it on a table in front of Dr. Weaver. The box contained a large glass jar holding the head of Bessie Little. On seeing the ghastly sight, Albert shuddered and turned his head. The skull, sliced in sections, sat on display as testimony to his deed.

The spectacle inside the courtroom was not the only one to note. As the procession carrying the head walked to the courtroom, it passed Miss Mollie Cart, a young woman Albert had been calling on and writing letters to while courting Bessie. They walked so close to her carrying the ghastly sight that she could not avert her gaze. She couldn't do anything but watch in terror as it was carried past.

Dr. Weaver described the second autopsy, which was performed at the request of Chief Farrell. Dr. J.M. Weaver, Fred's father, assisted in the autopsy. Dr. Weaver shared the grisly details of the examination of Bessie's head.

The body was dug up and removed from the wooden box. The skull was cut through and the top removed. As the outer layer of brain was punctured, liquid flowed out. This allowed him to see a hole just above the right ear, formerly obscured by dirt. Dr. Weaver then found pieces of lead inside the skull. Bessie's head was then removed and examined more thoroughly. Powder specks were evident along the edge of the wound, indicating the gun

Mollie Cart watched in horror as Bessie's head was carried past her.

had been shoved into her ear and fired. At this point, Dr. Weaver was asked to demonstrate the entrance and the path of the bullets in her head.

Rolling up his sleeves, Dr. Weaver reached into the jar of alcohol and took off the skin covering the skull. The pieces he removed were placed on blotters on the table. He lifted the skullcap, then the upper part of the head, then the lower part. He put the pieces back together on the table before him. With a piece of copper wire, he demonstrated the course of the bullets.

Death would have been instantaneous, Dr. Weaver explained. The upper end of the spinal column had been severed; therefore, she could not have controlled her muscular movement to be able to fire the second shot.

Engrossed in Dr. Weaver's testimony, Albert alternated between gruesome fascination and disgust. He grew nervous at the sight of Bessie's severed head but couldn't avert his eyes for long. He fixed his stare in every direction, but ultimately his gaze wandered right back to the head.

The stench in the courtroom was horrendous. Judge Brown had prepared in advance for this testimony and had an exhaust fan installed into the skylight above. The fan helped clear the air in the room but did not eliminate the odor completely. The windows had to be lowered to provide air circulation, and the jurors, sitting in front of the table, looked as if they wished they were anywhere else.

Suppressed excitement rippled through the courtroom during Dr. Weaver's testimony. The spectators in the room craned their necks and stood on their toes to see. Several times, Deputy Boes had to call for order in the courtroom, and many ladies coughed and covered their noses with handkerchiefs.

Bessie's head was removed from court, and Dr. Weaver was given a short break to go wash his hands. When he returned to the stand, Colonel Nevin asked him why he didn't examine the head during the first autopsy. Dr. Weaver explained that at the time, it was assumed that Bessie was pregnant and had committed suicide as a result. The first organ to be examined was the uterus, which showed she was not pregnant and had not been for at least a month. Next examined were her heart, lungs, liver, kidneys, etc., because the cavity was open. He gave several examples of instances where autopsies were performed and the head and brain were not examined. Before Dr. Fred Weaver finished his testimony, he identified the lead bullets taken from the skull.

Dr. J.M. Weaver, father to Dr. Fred Weaver and an experienced doctor, was the next witness. Dr. J.M. Weaver had been a surgeon for thirty-five years and had served as a surgeon in the army during the Civil War. He assisted his son Fred in the autopsies of Bessie Little. When asked if there was any special purpose in the first autopsy, he answered that it was to see if she was pregnant, which she was not. He then described the next autopsy, which was to examine the head. He found powder marks on the skin of the right ear and bullets in the brain. He explained the path of the lead and the damage it caused, noting that it would have caused death instantly. Dr. J.M. Weaver also explained that if the bullets had not killed instantly, they would have caused immediate unconsciousness.

Dr. Chrisman also assisted in the examination of the skull. He detailed removing the sawdust from the head in the cemetery and finding some sawdust embedded in the right ear. When removing the sawdust, he noted

Dr. J.M. Weaver, a veteran surgeon.

a bullet hole. Dr. Chrisman then described his further examination of the skull, repeating much of what both Dr. Weavers had stated. Dr. Chrisman told the jury that the bullet had gone directly through the medulla oblongata, which links the spinal cord to the brain. He agreed that death would have been instant, but that if Bessie had not died right away, she would have gone immediately unconscious. If Bessie had attempted suicide by shooting herself this way, she would not have been able to fire the gun twice.

Dr. Lee Corbin, coroner, detailed his official acts as coroner in the investigation. He mentioned the one witness who refused to testify at the coroner's inquest, which was Albert Frantz. He said Albert refused to testify at the instruction of Judge Kreitzer, who was enlisted as his legal counsel.

Corbin agreed with the testimony of the previous doctors who said death would have been instant if the first bullet passed through the medulla oblongata and that Bessie could not have shot herself twice. If the first bullet had not passed through the brain but had lodged between the skull and brain matter, as the defense argued, she would have immediately gone unconscious and still been unable to fire a second shot.

It was then that Colonel Nevin claimed the second autopsy was instigated when Albert sent word to coroner Corbin telling him he'd find bullets if he examined Bessie's head. Nevin argued that Albert wouldn't have sent word to Corbin if he wanted that information to be concealed.

Corbin corrected this claim. By the time Albert sent word to him, Chief Farrell had already had the body exhumed to be checked for a gunshot wound.

The court adjourned for lunch and continued in the afternoon. By the time the jailer walked Albert back into the courtroom, the crowd of women was the largest yet. With standing room only, two bailiffs had to hold the crowd back and admit them one by one.

Mrs. Elizabeth Little was recalled to the witness stand. In detail, she recounted getting Bessie from the Miami County Infirmary when Bessie was a toddler. She'd been abandoned by her birth parents, and the Littles didn't know who they were. They took her home and the family lived in

Troy for five years before moving to Dayton. They moved from May Street to Williams Street to Second Street to Home Avenue. They had been living on West Second Street for the past three years.

Elizabeth Little said Bessie and Albert met a year prior and he called on her frequently, often on a daily basis and no fewer than three times a week. Bessie never had any other company, and Bessie accepted as soon as Albert proposed, a fact one of Bessie's friends told Mrs. Little.

Mrs. Little had no issue with their relationship until she found Bessie and Albert in a compromising position in the barn behind their house. Bessie had gone to the barn and was gone for so long that Mrs. Little became suspicious. She went to the barn and found Frantz lying in the hay. When he finally rose from the hay, he said he meant no wrong and only secreted himself in the hay because he knew she'd object to his presence there. Albert begged Mrs. Little not to say anything to Mr. Little about the situation, but she refused to promise that. Albert stopped coming publicly to the house but would call on Bessie at night after Mr and Mrs. Little went to bed.

Mrs. Little claimed her sister heard a rumor that Albert wasn't going to marry Bessie, which prompted Mrs. Little to write a letter to Albert's father, telling him Bessie was "low born, of low origin" and "not the kind of girl any man would want to marry." She went on to say she was glad Bessie was not her child.

In July, Bessie went to call on Albert's father, and later that evening, Mrs. Little saw Bessie sitting in the yard crying and asked her what was wrong. Bessie told her mother that she went to the Frantz house to ask Mr. Frantz to allow Albert to marry her and he said no. Albert had promised her he would marry her, and she wanted to get him to sign a paper stating he would.

Mrs. Little told Bessie that if she continued to see Albert, she would have to leave the house. Later, she called on Bessie at the Hotel Cooper in response to a letter from Bessie asking her to visit. Bessie had heard rumors that Albert might not marry her and wanted to talk to Mrs. Little about them. Mrs. Little then claimed she received a letter from one of Albert's relatives confirming that Albert would not be marrying Bessie.

Mr. Peter Little took the stand next and told the story of the time he discovered Albert standing outside the kitchen door with his shoes off.

I heard a noise at the door and opening it, discovered a man on the outside steps with his shoes off. I said "Hello there! What are you doing here?" It was Frantz and he replied that he was there to see Bessie. I told him we expected visitors to ring when calling. He turned and disappeared in the darkness, leaving his shoes behind. The shoes are still at my house.

Bessie had been sleeping on a bed lounge downstairs in the dining room. This was the night of the episode in the barn, and Mrs. Little had moved her upstairs. Frantz had no reason to suppose that she was not still in the dining room that night, occupying the bed lounge.

Mr. Little told Albert never to visit the home again. He believed Bessie left the Little's home because Albert was no longer allowed to visit her there. He told another story about the time he ran into Bessie with Albert on St. Clair Street after she left home. He asked her to return home, and she said she didn't care to do so.

The bookkeeper at the Hotel Cooper, Mrs. Amanda Bell, said Bessie registered at the hotel on July 25. Mrs. Bell didn't meet Bessie until nearly a week later. She didn't meet Albert until several days later when he stopped by to call for Bessie. Albert told Mrs. Bell that Bessie had been forced out of the house so her parents could make room for other relatives to stay there and that he couldn't afford to marry her yet. He asked Mrs. Bell not to register Bessie, as he didn't want her parents or anyone else to be able to find her there. Mrs. Bell found the relationship between Bessie and Albert to be unusual and later asked Albert why he didn't just marry her. He said he would not be forced to marry anyone.

Mrs. Bell said she knew of a letter Bessie wrote to Albert's father. She sent the letter through a bellboy named Howard Hughes. The next day, Albert called on Bessie at the hotel. He was angry and made a scene, telling Mrs. Bell that Bessie had written a letter to his father making serious charges and causing him a lot of trouble at home. In the letter, Bessie urged Mr. Frantz to right the wrong by allowing Albert to marry her. Albert paid Bessie's bill and said he was done with her. He stormed up the stairs to her room and came down a bit later and left. Not long after, Mrs. Bell heard a rumor that Albert had bought a revolver on August 13. When she later read in the newspaper about a body found in the river, she called Albert and asked him to come to the hotel and talk to her. Someone was standing nearby when he arrived, so she asked him about the fire in his barn, and he responded, "Yes, we'll not take any more buggy rides."

As the third party walked away from them, Mrs. Bell asked where Bessie was, and Albert said he didn't know. Mrs. Bell offered to call on Bessie's parents and he told her not to, that he'd just come from Mrs. Freese's boardinghouse and she said she would go. Mrs. Bell urged Albert to notify the police.

While Bessie was staying at the Hotel Cooper, Mrs. Bell said, she was a perfect lady and well-liked by everyone at the hotel. At night, she was sad and fearful, often heard pacing the floor in her room and crying. Bessie's moods were controlled by Albert, and he could make her laugh or cry at his will.

Bessie confided in Mrs. Bell that Albert told her he was arranging for a reconciliation between her and her parents and he would soon be allowed to call on her at her house again. She had never seen Bessie any happier in the time she knew her. Bessie left that evening with Albert and returned the next morning looking devastated. Bessie was so sad that simply being around her made Mrs. Bell feel sad as well. That was the day Bessie wrote the letter to Albert's father.

Bessie once told Mrs. Bell that she had considered suicide. One Sunday, while she was crossing the Third Street Bridge in a streetcar, she thought about jumping into the water below, as its level was very high at the time.

Mrs. Minnie Freese was next to testify. She said Bessie registered at her boardinghouse on August 20 and said Albert was going to pay her board. They both told Mrs. Freese they were to be married on October 28. They told her this just a few days before Bessie's death. On August 27, Bessie left the boardinghouse at 6:10 p.m., walked north on Jefferson to Fifth Street and turned east on Fifth Street. That was the last time Mrs. Freese saw Bessie.

Albert showed up at the boardinghouse on August 28 around 9:00 a.m. and stayed half an hour. He had a different suit on than the light suit he normally wore. Mrs. Freese remembered that specifically, as she thought he must not have been working that day, since she knew he owned better clothing.

During that time, Mrs. Freese asked Albert where Bessie was, and he said he didn't know. When Mrs. Freese said Bessie went out to see him the night before, Albert told her she was mistaken, but Mrs. Freese told him she was not. He said, "Why Mrs. Freese, I did not see her last evening, I saw her yesterday afternoon. What should I want to see her again for in the evening?"

Albert insisted he pay four dollars for a week's board in advance for Bessie. He also told Mrs. Freese that he couldn't marry Bessie until October, when he received his inheritance from his mother.

By then it was well past 5:00 p.m., so court adjourned for the day.

Another prisoner in the same area of the jail as Albert approached him that day and said to him, "You killed Bessie." It turned out he was Bessie's cousin, a young man named Rawlins. When Rawlins said this, Albert turned pale and asked another prisoner, "You won't go back on me, will you?"

FRIDAY, DECEMBER 18, 1896

By 8:00 a.m., the crowd of spectators had begun gathering in the corridors of the courthouse just to get a glimpse of Albert. As he walked to the courthouse, the crowd split to make way for him. After he entered the courtroom, the onlookers followed, pushing themselves in as much as the bailiffs would allow.

Mrs. Freese was recalled to the stand. She spoke of a conversation with Albert two days after Bessie's death about his barn. Albert told Mrs. Freese that his barn had been burned and his horse was killed. She asked him how it happened, and he said he didn't know, then asked her if she thought he had done it. He said he went into the barn and attempted to free his horse, but he fell and needed to get out to save himself. He told her he cried the next morning when he saw his horse.

Albert said he would return the next day to see if Bessie had come back but next called on her several days later. When Mrs. Freese said she would call at the Little home to see if Bessie was there, Albert said Mrs. Little wouldn't even let her in. Mrs. Freese said she would call on the Littles; then, after being allowed into the home, she would ask about Bessie. However, she wasn't able to go.

Mrs. Freese spoke of the day Albert came to register Bessie at her boardinghouse. Bessie had picked a different room because it was cheaper, but Albert came in to check the rooms and picked one he liked better. Bessie remained in the buggy while Albert checked the room. He said it did not make any difference which room it was, because Bessie would not be the one to pay for it. He asked Mrs. Freese to watch her closely and try to divert her mind from trouble. He said that at the Hotel Cooper, Bessie had to be watched closely for fear she would commit suicide.

One night, while Bessie was staying at her boardinghouse, the couple was together, and Mrs. Freese heard someone crying. She asked Bessie about it later, and Bessie said it was Albert who was crying. She said she didn't believe Albert intended to marry her and she planned to return to her parents' home and not marry him. Mrs. Freese's husband also heard Albert sobbing. Another boarder staying in an upstairs room looked out the window when he heard crying and saw Bessie and Albert sitting on the steps together.

Mrs. Freese said Bessie often cried and walked the floor at night, wringing her hands. She thought Bessie was really homesick and she feared that after Albert got his legacy, he wouldn't marry her. Once, in a fit of anger, Bessie told Mrs. Freese she would not marry Albert.

The public showed up en masse to Albert's trial every day.

When asked if she knew Bessie was pregnant, Mrs. Freese answered that she knew Bessie was not pregnant and claimed to have evidence to partially prove that she was not, implying Bessie had been having periods during her stay at the boardinghouse.

Russell Elliot, an expert chemist, brought a set of very fine scales to weigh the leaden bullets that came from Bessie's head. He weighed the pieces, together and separately, in front of the jury. The total weight of the lead was 172 grains, and separately, the pieces weighed $14\frac{1}{2}$, $73\frac{1}{2}$, $60\frac{3}{4}$ and 36 grains, equaling $184\frac{3}{4}$ grains. Elliot explained that when it came to such small weights, there was likely to be a discrepancy. He said a .32-caliber bullet was supposed to weigh 86 grains.

John Poince had worked at Dodd's Gun Store for nearly two years when Albert came in to buy a revolver. He confirmed Albert bought a .32-caliber Forehand & Wadsworth revolver and a box of cartridges on August 13. He was in and out of the store in ten minutes. Pounce identified Albert as the man who bought the gun in his store that day and the man who was brought to his house to be identified.

Poince said he always got a good look at customers when he sold weapons to them. The defense heard this statement and asked Poince if he'd be able to identify a man who bought a gun from him within the last ten days. Without his glasses, Poince was unable to see clearly. He looked around the room,

The pistol buyer, whom Poince could not identify in the crowd.

looking from face to face, his eyes resting on each face momentarily then moving to the next. For ten minutes, he looked around the courtroom, studying and squinting at each face, until finally he gave up, announcing he did not recognize anyone in the courtroom as having bought a weapon from him in the past ten days. Seconds later, a man walked quietly out of the courtroom, his identity kept a secret.

Attorney Kumler wanted to pass a revolver around to the jurors to let them test to see how easy it would be to pull the trigger. The defense objected, and the gun was not passed around, as it was not the same type used to shoot Bessie. Eventually, Kumler argued his way into handing the gun to each juryman and having him snap the trigger.

William Kissinger was a clerk at the Hotel Cooper and knew Albert from having seen him pay Bessie's bill. He later saw Albert in the gun store on August 13; he remembered the date because it was the day before the Cincinnati Reds played in Dayton. He saw Albert at the corner of Fourth and Main. Albert was walking ahead of him, and he could clearly see him walk into Dodd's Gun Store.

John Henry lived approximately two hundred to three hundred yards north of the bridge and fifty yards west of the river and heard a scream that night. He was at home with his daughter on the evening of August 27 when he heard a woman scream and two shots coming from the direction of the bridge. The scream came first, closely followed by the shots. Henry fixed the time somewhere between 7:00 and 8:00 p.m., before dark.

William Sigler (also spelled Ziegler) was a porter at the Beckel House who lived near the Soldiers Home, along the White Line tracks. Sigler was one of the young men who found Bessie's side combs the day after her death. He was walking along the bridge on August 28 between 6:30 and 7:00 p.m. when he saw a side comb and blood on the north side of the bridge. There were several blood spots near the side comb, the largest four inches around. The blood was still fresh. Sigler turned the comb over to the police.

John Herby was tending to his horse when he heard two shots, one then another in quick succession. He lived near the Stillwater bridge and said shots were not uncommon in that area.

PHRENOLOGY

A phrenologist was called to the stand to give his opinion on Albert's appearance and personality. Phrenology was the detailed study of the shape and size of the cranium as indicators of personality traits and mental abilities. Although the practice has been widely discredited in modern times, it helped inspire research on localization of parts of the brain and their functions, laying the groundwork for the development of neurology.

Directly from the *Kentucky Post and Times-Star*, Professor Stone gave the following report:

> *In examining the physiology of Albert Frantz, I first note that the base of his skull is comparatively much too broad, deep and heavy for the upper portion of the head, thus linking him to tastes and interests of a low order,*

and just the reverse of what would be manifest had the upper part, with its moral tendency, been duly developed.

Therefore, these ennobling faculties not generating sufficient strength to counterbalance the lower ones, the based passions would necessarily run riot. The crown of the head would require much more height, breadth, and fullness to successfully combat the lower tendencies of mind.

These unrestrained passions in their excessive activity would eventually become disordered under a continuous and false excitement, and become consequently incapable through their habitual excesses of resisting still greater temptation to a vicious course of life.

What may often appear from its unrestrained fury as insanity, if judged from results, is in reality but the outgrowth of a perverted nature, given over to and gloating upon the more vulgar elements of life. But as any vital organs become too long and actively engaged in its operations, so it is also with the brain, and its respective functions.

There may become so gradually disordered as to blot out all distinct lines or demarcation between sanity and insanity. And like a superheated steam boiler when not relieved of its dangerous pressure, ultimately results in a terrific explosion, destroying everything in its course.

His forehead is too low, narrow and contracted, manifesting a nature impervious to purifying and sympathetic feelings, thus disposing him to great selfishness, ingratitude, and skepticism and thus not amenable to those kindly influences which dispose one to overlook trifling mistakes in others, but with his coarse, stiff, wiry hair growing well down toward the forehead and his stiff bushy eyebrows, he would be disposed to look upon the dark rather than the brighter side of life. Thus he would be disposed to nurse a morose rather than a cheery, genial frame of mind.

As his eyebrows are close to the eye and the forehead strongly projects over eyes which are restless and watchful, he would be a very close observer of those about, with his penetrating mind, would dispose him to note very closely and retain things that he was seeking after and dispose him to an irritable impatient mood and strong suspicions, and a lack of strong social feeling and a feeling of general reserve and mistrust.

He has a very cold and furtive glitter in the eye that would dispose him to be very suspicious and watchful of the tricks and catches of life, and thus lack a warm cordiality and freedom of expression. But his eye has also that peculiarly dead cavernous hard, steely, glitter denoting a strong criminal undercurrent of feeling, yet requiring unusual circumstances to set it aflame, and never ordinary conditions when once allowed to smolder, thus

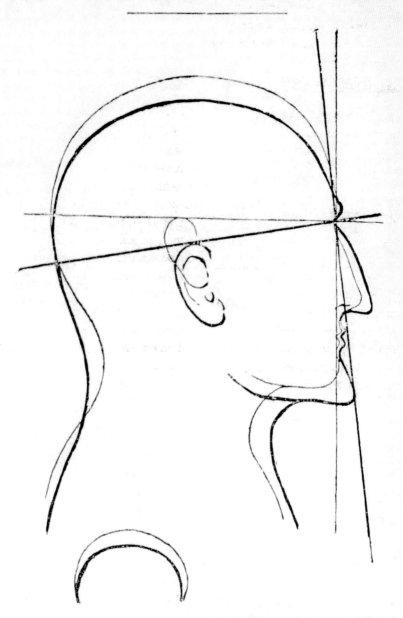

The ratio of Albert's eyes, ears and brow was said to indicate an irritable mood and lack of social feeling.

allowing one of his nature to live for years under assumed respectability until his great resentment of vindictiveness overcomes his caution and drives him restlessly forth to extreme violences, as he would brook no apparition to his desires or passions.

But this expression of eye, as also many features of criminal instincts, is more readily discerned than described by trained observers, becoming eventually as it were an instinct with him, but incapable of exact description or definition.

He has a very long, protruding, square and massive chin, the entire lower portion of his face in fact projecting beyond the normal perpendicular line of the average countenance.

His jaws are also broad, heavy and square, this entire portion of the face being coarse and forbidding, all indicating an excessive predominance of the lower propensities over the more elevating sentiments, and an unbridled sensuality, selfishness, and jealousy, with great propelling power or energy, which would like a surging, seething, torrent impel him to tear away every obstruction in his course, leaving devastation behind.

He has very long, wiry fingers, which lack soft, supple expression, as each phalanx is too straight and rigid in each structure, with a too tightly drawn skin, which, when slightly bent, leaving conjunction, with a constant and rigid hooking of the thumb, gives a clawlike expression of the hand.

This would denote a grasping, impatient, arbitrary, and insatiable nature, inclining him to magnify and brood over trifling matters, though not sufficiently to cause his great vitality and recuperative power to seriously derange his mind, he having rather a cool and calculating disposition, though under a great temper it may become temporarily deranged.

His nose is very long, massive, irregular, and hook shape, somewhat resembling a beak, with a turn-down tip, which, with his peculiarly small

THE FOREHEAD.

The shape of Albert's forehead indicated a selfish and ungrateful nature, according to Professor Stone.

BROW AND EYE.

Albert's "peculiarly dead" eyes.

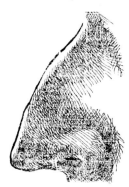

A PROMINENT NOSE.

Albert's nose, described as "beak-like."

A sketch of Albert's head, which the phrenologist used to study the shapes and outlines of his features.

and closely set eyes, give a remarkably close resemblance to the piercing, soaring, untamable eagle, and would in like manner, manifest many of its qualities and like it, take one unawares and strike suddenly and scarcely defend himself when driven to bay.

For a summary I will use an outline profile view of the head of Albert Frantz. In comparing line of Frantz with those of the lighter or standard head and face, it can be readily observed the striking inferiority of Frantz's head. The lack of height of head and forehead above the line running over the top of the ear, which lies very close to the center of [the] *brain and from which we judge indicates a low character. Here can also be noted the great projection of the lower face, which denotes harsh, sensual passions protruding far beyond the lighter perpendicular line of moral restraint.*

The reader should note the excessive depth of ear below the horizontal line, running through profile, and the long, massive bony development of the square chin and jaw. Beneath this line, all denoting a harsh stubborn self-will, selfishness, vindictiveness. Then the long thick irregular hooked nose and thick puffy neck also denote licentious tastes and fierce ungovernable destructive temper.

Frantz also has commendable characteristics. The projecting brow denotes keen observation and good, general intelligence. His small mouth and well center of lips, a quiet approachable and unaffected nature. The curve beneath the lower lip shows good, respectable parentage, and artistic tastes, though uncultivated and occasional spells of repentance, while his clear, smooth skin and clear cut lines denote an attention to work, good general memory, a fair degree of courtesy and capacity for improvement were he not so selfish, obstinate, jealous, and so readily blinded by his passion and spiteful temper.

—Professor Stone, phrenologist and physiognomist

Chapter 8

THE TRIAL: WE SAW YOU

Saturday, December 19, 1896

Rumors that Albert was to take the stand on his sixth day of court had the courtroom packed earlier than ever. Once the room was filled and the doors were closed, over one thousand people had been turned away. Deputy Sheriff Wood and court bailiff Boes struggled to handle the women, who tried to run them over in attempts to get into the building. Deputy Wood said he'd prefer to handle a crowd of men on election day rather than ladies at a murder trial.

Just before the start of court, defense lawyers sought information from newspaper reporters from Cincinnati and Northern Kentucky regarding the story of Henry Van Doren, who shot himself three times in the head in an attempt to commit suicide. The defense was looking into the case as precedent to show that someone might be able to shoot themselves multiple times in the head. Van Doren had locked himself in a room and shot himself twice in the forehead and once in the right side of the head. Astoundingly, he was alive when police found him, and he survived the ordeal.

The trial resumed with more talk of the side combs found on the bridge.

Frank Ross of 203 South Williams Street said he and William Sigler were on the bridge when they found the combs and the clusters of blood spots on the ground. The spots covered an area of two to three feet. Each witness found one comb and identified them in the courtroom.

William Sigler and Frank Ross, who found Bessie's side combs.

Charles Shellabarger, ex-councilman and a foreman stonecutter, was at the bridge on Labor Day and found a hair on the bridge rail. He climbed over the rail and found a number of other hairs, which were long and brown. He pulled them off one at a time, and members of the crowd grabbed them from his hands as souvenirs. He was able to keep a few strands and turned them over to the police.

Jeanette Herby, daughter of the previous day's witness John Herby, testified she heard a woman's screams followed by gunshots on the night of August 27. The scream was long and loud, followed by a short silence before two revolver shots resounded. Miss Herby was certain the shots were from a revolver and not a gun because, she said, shots from a revolver were much louder than shots from a gun. The sounds all came from the direction of the bridge, but she could not see anything specific, as it was getting dark.

Martin Dobb lived three-quarters of a mile south of the bridge and also heard shots from the direction of the bridge on the night of August 27. He fixed the time of the sounds around dark.

C.M. McCrea, office partner to George Mannix, the attorney boarding in the room next to Bessie at the Hotel Cooper, was next to take the stand. He testified to establish the date of a telephone message for Mannix from a Mr. Totton in Cincinnati.

George Mannix was called next. He had an office in the Callahan Bank Building and kept board at the Hotel Cooper in August. He stayed in the room next to Bessie and recounted her behavior, crying and praying at night about a dozen times. He said she always seemed melancholy but sometimes had bright spells. Mannix was receiving the phone call from Mr. Totton when he overheard Albert talking to Mrs. Bell, telling her he would not be forced to marry Bessie.

William Brenneman, cashier at the Central Union Telephone Company, had the record of charge for the long-distance call to George Mannix.

Amy Crawford, a Central Union Telephone Company operator, had a record of the charge for service over the long-distance line for C.M. McCrea, showing he received a certain telephone message from George Mannix on August 13.

Mrs. Mary Ryan, telephone operator, testified to a certain bill for telephone service that was made out by her to George Mannix on August 13 from Cornelius McGillicuddy (Connie Mack, of Pittsburgh baseball fame).

Walter Regan, who lived at 1626 West Second Street, was a neighbor to Bessie and a coworker to Albert. He recalled seeing Albert sneaking into the barn behind the Little house twice. He saw Albert call at the Little house after Mr. and Mrs. Little went to bed. He fixed the date as July 11. Albert tapped lightly on the side door, took off his shoes, coat, vest and hat and laid them on the step. He then entered the house, stayed for an hour and left the house in a hurry, grabbing his clothing off the porch as he ran away. The next night was the same, but Albert stayed in the house for two hours before leaving.

Several days later, on July 17, Mr. Regan saw Albert sneaking around the house and threw open his shutters, asking Albert what he was doing there so late at night. Albert had his shoes in his hand and ran away. He came back a few hours later, removed his shoes again and hid them in some vines. Mr. Regan ran over to the Little house and rang the bell, alerting Mr. Little, who took Albert's shoes and kept them. Mr. Regan said it was April when he first saw Albert sneaking around the Little residence, and the night Albert couldn't get in, he sat on the steps for about twenty minutes, head in hands, and audibly groaned twice.

Mrs. Regan, Walter Regan's wife, also knew of the clandestine relationship between Albert and Bessie. One night she saw Bessie go into the alley and motion for Albert to go away. She described a noise Albert and Bessie used to signal each other; she called it "perting." Mrs. Regan attempted to imitate the sound, making a noise with her lips and tongue.

On July 17, Mrs. Regan saw Albert meet Bessie in the barn and, watching them through a crack in the fence, saw them lying in the hay together. Moments later she saw Mrs. Little go into the barn, and she heard Albert ask Mrs. Little not to talk so loudly and not to tell anyone what she saw.

Mrs. Regan repeated the same story her husband told about the nights Albert entered the house after the Littles went to bed, leaving his coat, vest, hat and shoes on the porch while he went inside.

FRANTZ'S SIGNAL.
The "Pert," to Which Bessie Little Responded.

The tune of Albert and Bessie's signal.

Mrs. Regan was asked if she knew of any signs that Bessie was pregnant, and Mrs. Regan said she had a conversation with Bessie about the subject after seeing her vomiting in the yard. She was not allowed to share what was said in the conversation, as it was considered hearsay.

Sol Strauss, a Third Street clothing dealer, testified that the pieces of clothing found in the barn were similar to goods he had in his store. He did not know Albert. He was asked if the clothing was bought in his store but was not allowed to answer.

Noah Brookins lived next door to Albert and worked with him at the Mathias Planing Mill. He said he knew Albert to be a stenographer and a collector for the company. Albert wrote all the letters for the company at Brookins's dictation. Albert spent half his working time out collecting debts for the company.

Albert was on duty on August 27 and 28. He typically wore a light-colored suit to work, which he had said he got from the clothing store owned by Sol Strauss. The day after the barn fire, Albert was wearing a dark-colored suit. He told Brookins his light-colored suit burned in the barn fire. Brookins was able to identify the pieces of cloth from the fire as pieces of the suit.

Brookins had known Bessie for at least a decade before her death. He had spoken to Albert about his relationship with Bessie, and Albert told him an attempt was being made to force him to marry her. Albert had made up his mind to leave the city but later decided against it, fearing Bessie would get the inheritance money that was coming to him.

When Brookins brought up the neighborhood gossip regarding the couple, Albert denied having an illicit relationship with Bessie and said he did not intend to marry her. Albert told Brookins he thought Bessie was going to do to him all the damage she could and ruin his reputation.

Brookins was at home the evening of the fire. He saw Albert running from the back of the Frantz yard to the barn, yelling, "Fire! Fire!" loudly. When he looked, he saw that the front part of the barn was burned away, and he could hear noises in the barn that sounded like the horse trying to get loose. Brookins ran to the nearest fire box to call in the fire but first needed to retrieve a fire key from a nearby grocery store. When he returned to the box, Mrs. Fromme had already opened the box and pulled the hook.

Mrs. Myrtle Chapman lived across the street from the Frantz residence and the Brookins residence. When she first saw the fire at the Frantz barn, she was in her home. She ran across the street into Mr. Brookins's yard to where Mrs. Brookins and Albert were standing. She asked if the fire engines had arrived yet, but they gave no answer. Albert said he hadn't thought of it yet. When Mrs. Chapman told Albert he'd better call or his entire barn would burn down, Albert said he guessed so but did not walk away to call. Later, Mrs Chapman went into the Frantz yard and heard Albert comment that there were too many people in his yard; he fetched a police officer to make them all leave.

Frank McBride, a Dayton police detective, testified next. He described going out to the Frantz residence to examine the burned barn, where he found part of a buggy and pieces of a man's vest. He was able to identify the lining of the vest as what he found in the barn that day. His testimony was corroborated by E.S. Fair of the police department.

Detective Steve Perry was at the scene of the burned barn and searched the ruins. He made three visits to the scene. He took parts of the burned buggy to police headquarters.

Special Officer Clayton picked up a piece of cloth from the vest near one of the rear buggy axles and identified it in court.

W.A. Cugel, police operator, was out with other officers searching the ruins. He also identified the cloth found.

Court adjourned for the day at noon.

Sunday, December 20, 1896

The jurors were supposed to attend Sunday service at the First Reformed Church in the morning, but they were unable to do so since two of them were sick. Mr. James Daugherty suffered from "severe cramp colic and sick headache," and Mr. Isaac Haynes, an older gentleman, was suffering from the confinement of jury duty. The group was also supposed to take a car ride via the Traction Line to Miamisburg and return in the afternoon, but this was canceled as well. Instead, they spent the day at the Hotel Cooper reading and talking among themselves.

Monday, December 21, 1896

The trial resumed with women in mass attendance once again. The ladies ranged from young and giddy girls to matronly-looking housewives and even some grandmothers. The number of women was so notable to a reporter from the *Dayton Herald* that he mentioned it in his article on December 21, 1896:

Just what special interest attaches to Frantz that should attract such a lot of wives, mothers, and daughters, is a mystery, unless it be that the prisoner is charged with murder. It is a notorious fact that women exhibit more morbid curiosity in a man charged with a capital offense than they do in anything else. And so, when Court Officer Boes by direction of Judge Brown, opened court at 9 am, the seats in the rear of the rail which separates the spectators from the witness, were well filled with women. Indeed, there were more women in these seats than men, and the wonder of it all is that many of them were women of well-known respectability.

Albert arrived to court early, in the charge of Sheriff Anderton and Jailer Wood. Jailer Wood had been by Albert's side almost continuously for the entirety of the trial. When Jailer Wood was called away, Sheriff Anderton took his place. Jacob Frantz was seated behind and to the left of Albert. The elder Frantz had trouble getting around and required the use of a crutch. Family brought him to court every morning and afternoon, and they made great efforts to ensure his comfort during the proceedings. Along with Albert's father, many members of the Frantz family and the Dunkard community showed up each day.

Opening court, Chief Farrell recited his involvement in the case, starting from very little knowledge of a woman who was found floating in the river, through identifying her, tracing her last movements, searching the river for the revolver and tracking the evidence to make the case against Albert. It was an impressive tale, and many became admirers of his work.

Fire chief Dan Larkin was next to take the stand. Larkin had been fire chief for seventeen years and was also secretary of the fire board. He brought a record of the Frantz fire with him. It said: "August 28, evening, Box 75, frame stable, rear of 1609 West Second Street, estate of D.L. Rike & Co. Loss on Building $75; on contents $160. Cause of fire: Incendiarism" (arson).

Albert Honacker, a friend of Albert Frantz, lived at the corner of King Street and Home Avenue. Honacker was present at the barn fire at the Frantz residence. He first noticed Albert Frantz running around in just his shirtsleeves. Honacker said he had to run several "squares" (blocks) to get to the Frantz residence and see the fire. When he got there, the barn door was open and he could see the horse inside. The fire had reached the buggy but not the horse. Honaker attempted to go toward the barn to rescue the horse. He could have reached him and gotten him out safely, but Albert Frantz stopped him, saying he would not allow anyone to risk their life for a horse.

Albert was escorted into court in the charge of Sheriff Anderton and Jailer Wood.

James McDonald was next. McDonald saw a man running around in shirtsleeves but did not know him. McDonald witnessed the man in shirtsleeves preventing Honacker from entering the barn to save the horse.

George Grice noticed smoke and was the first to arrive at the fire. When he arrived, Albert was not there; he didn't arrive until three minutes later in his shirtsleeves, carrying an ax. Grice wanted to tear down the barn door, but Albert refused to give him the ax he was holding. Grice stated that if Albert had given him the ax, he could have gotten into the barn and saved the horse and buggy with plenty of time.

George Nicholas of 1641 West Second Street was also at the fire. His attention was caught when he heard a woman cry out, "My God, the horse!" The woman was seated in a buggy in front of the Frantz house. Nicholas ran to the barn and opened the front door. The fire seemed to be confined to the buggy. The fire department was there at the time.

Dr. O.E. Francis, a West Side physician, examined Bessie at Albert's request on July 16. Dr. Francis was the reason Bessie thought she was pregnant. Dr. Francis assumed that Bessie's symptoms of nausea meant she was with child. Albert hinted at asking for a pill to induce miscarriage, but Dr. Francis refused. Instead, he prescribed medicine to settle Bessie's stomach.

The couple visited Dr. Francis again a week later. Again, he examined Bessie and diagnosed her as pregnant. The couple together called on Dr. Francis a third, fourth and fifth time, each visit getting the same result.

Mrs. Anna Claude lived two houses west of the Little home and had witnessed Bessie and Albert secretly meeting. She had often heard a "perting" sound, sometimes a few times a day. When asked what the "perting" sounded like, she referred to the birdlike trill Mrs. Regan made when she testified, eliciting laughter throughout the courtroom.

The court took a recess for lunch.

When the trial resumed that afternoon, James Moore was the first witness called to the stand. Moore lived in Riverdale near the bridge. Along with his friend John Roof, he was in the vicinity of the bridge on August 27. Both men heard two shots around 7:30 p.m.

Matilda Lynam (sister-in-law to Lee Lynam, Dayton's first police officer killed in the line of duty) saw Albert on the evening of August 27 driving east on First Street from Euclid Street after supper.

Elsie Puterbaugh, the fourteen-year-old niece of Mr. and Mrs. Little, was living with the Littles before Bessie left their home. Elsie slept downstairs and once saw Albert visiting Bessie at night. Albert often visited Bessie on Thursday afternoons when Mrs. Little was not home. One afternoon, they went upstairs at one o'clock and did not come back down until four.

Claude Eichelberger was in a streetcar on Mechanic Street when he saw Albert on the evening of August 27. Albert was in a buggy ahead of the streetcar and turned east on Fifth Street down the boulevard.

Mrs. Laura Nichols, sister of Mrs. Little, testified she saw Albert one evening in late August and asked him where Bessie was. Albert replied he didn't know, and Nichols said it was his duty to know since they were engaged. Albert disagreed: he and Bessie weren't engaged, he said.

Miss Ella Crowell, a schoolteacher, saw Bessie get on a Fifth Street car westbound on the evening of August 27. Bessie got on at Jefferson and went west.

Dunkard minister William Teeter was next. Teeter was not sworn in due to his faith but instead affirmed (an affirmation has the same legal effect as an oath but without the religious implications). Teeter had been a minister since 1878. The first time he met Albert was August 27, 1896, when Albert came to his Horace Street home around 9:30 p.m. Teeter was home with his wife, Phoebe, when they heard a knock at the door. It was Albert, Phoebe's first cousin. They invited him inside.

Albert had a haggard expression on his face as he pushed past them both, walked through the kitchen, then threw himself onto a chair in their sitting room. When they asked him what was wrong, Albert cried out, "Oh, my God, what shall I do, what shall I do?"

Again, they asked him what was wrong. Albert exclaimed, "Oh, if she had only done it on a public street or where someone could have seen it."

He then fainted, and the Teeters had trouble reviving him. When he finally came around, he told them Bessie planned a drive, he met her on the boulevard and they drove out through Riverdale. Albert said Bessie wanted to go out to the new bridge near where a boat sank recently. When they were on the bridge, he said, Bessie told him, "Now you look down that way, and I'll look up this way, and we will see if we can see anything."

Reverend W.C. Teeters on the stand.

Albert then claimed that while his head was turned away from her, he heard two shots and immediately knew Bessie had shot herself. His horse plunged madly, and he could barely control it. Albert then said he thought he'd be suspected of murder and, reacting in fear, threw Bessie's body into the river, tossing the revolver in after her. When Teeter asked how Bessie got the revolver, Albert said she asked for money earlier in

Reverend Isaac Frantz, Albert's brother.

the week for stockings and clothes and he gave her five dollars. He assumed she used the money to buy the revolver.

Teeter told Albert he made a mistake with each toss into the river. In response, Albert threatened to go back to the bridge and drown himself in the river. Teeter advised Albert to seek legal advice and send for his brother Isaac, another Dunkard minister. Together, Teeter and Albert wrote a letter to Isaac and, instead of mailing it, sent Phoebe to Mount Pleasant to deliver the note the next morning. Isaac called on Albert later the same day, and together the men went to Judge Kreitzer to seek legal advice. Isaac wanted to go to the police with the information about Bessie's death, but Kreitzer told them to wait and let matters take their own course.

Reverend Isaac Frantz was next to testify. After he was affirmed (not sworn in), Isaac corroborated the information from Teeter. Isaac told Albert that guilty or not, he ought to notify the authorities. Albert turned to him and said, "Why Isaac, do you think I could be so cruel as to murder poor Bessie?"

Isaac delivered the story with much feeling, his voice choking with emotion as he described the conversation with his baby brother. He begged Judge Kreitzer to allow him to tell the story, but Kreitzer told him to hold his peace and wait. Isaac begged Albert to come forward with the information about Bessie's death, but Albert was too afraid of being arrested.

After court was adjourned, Chief Farrell; newspaper reporter W.A. Stuart; newspaper correspondents Karl Landon, Ed Anthony and W.J. Taylor; and detectives McBride and Niedergal drove out to the bridge where Bessie met her fate. The group went to the Herby residence, where John and Jeanette Herby claimed to have been when they heard two shots and a scream, while Chief Farrell and reporter Stuart stayed at the bridge. Farrell screamed three times from different positions and fired two shots. Not only did the witnesses at the Herby residence hear the screams and shots, but they also saw the flash of the gun. The tests proved the validity of their claims.

Chapter 9

THE TRIAL: MOLLIE CART

TUESDAY, DECEMBER 22, 1896

As the jurors made their way along the snow-covered path from the Hotel Cooper, many commented on "the snow, the snow, the beautiful snow."

Some of the older men acted like young boys, giving court officer Boes a lot to handle as he ushered them into the courthouse. Meanwhile, Deputies Wood and Bozenhard struggled to control the massive crowd of women pressing their way into court. The snow had slowed the crowds, and for the first time since the trial started, there were a few empty seats in the courtroom.

Albert looked the worst he'd ever looked that morning as he made his way into court. It was clear he hadn't been sleeping or eating well, and the strain was evident on his face. His cheeks had lost color and shape. Despite that, he appeared to take pleasure in the bit of snow dusting his route. He detoured off the beaten path to take a few steps in the quarter-inch-deep snow, leaving his footprints behind. His pointed shoes were two-and-a-half inches wide and eleven-and-a-quarter inches long. His stride was nineteen inches in length, and he walked in a calm and confident manner.

The first witness in court that day was the one everyone had been waiting for: Mollie Cart, the other woman. Mollie was a pretty brunette of medium height. She was well dressed, wearing a dark street dress with a tailor-made sacque, or jacket. She was from Trotwood, far enough away for Albert to be able to keep his intentions toward her a secret from Bessie. Albert had called

FRANTZ'S FOOTPRINTS.

Albert's footprints in the snow.

on her frequently over the prior two years, especially from March to late July 1896. He had even proposed to her in March, but she refused him. His last visit to her was in July. She considered him a dear friend.

Mollie had received several letters from Albert over the spring and summer and identified them in court. Before they were entered into evidence, the letters were turned over to the defense attorneys for inspection. A delay ensued when copies of the letters were made for the defense. Once court resumed, Mollie was called back to the stand.

The first letter was dated March 19, 1896, and was addressed to "My Dear Mollie." In that letter, Albert promised to call on her at her request. Throughout the letter, he called her "my dear" and closed by saying, "I must get my breakfast, tata." He said he would leave her with a kiss.

The next letter, postmarked April 15, was written on stationery with a "Mathias Planing Mill" heading on top. Albert mentioned he had been sick and was glad he was well and able to work. He'd heard Mollie was mad at him, and he apologized for disappointing her.

Albert asked Mollie how her Easter was and indicated that his was not enjoyable. He asked her how many eggs she ate; he had none. He thanked her for an Easter card she sent him and suggested that in the spirit of leap year, she visit him. He closed the letter with: "Goodbye, with a kiss, I remain as ever, yours. Bert."

During the reading of this particular letter, Albert had trouble holding back the tears. Before the reading of the letters continued, the prosecution asked Mollie who her "regular company" was. The defense objected but was overruled. Mollie answered, "Albert Frantz."

The third letter was postmarked May 8 and began with: "Dear Friend Mollie, neglected, not forgotten my dear." Albert apologized for not writing to her promptly and said he was writing her from Miamisburg, as he had thirty minutes' train time to do so. He said he intended to hire someone to write correspondence for him and asked her if she'd like to do it. After he asked her how many parties she was attending, he signed with: "Write soon dear, for I enjoy your letters. B."

The next letter, written on May 19, started with "My Dear Mollie" then said, "Why my dear, you get tired of housekeeping very quick. What are you going to do after marriage?" Albert commented he'd better go to Salt Lake and become a Mormon. He denied some rumors Mollie had heard about him and commented that people should hold their tongues. This letter was signed, "With a kiss, remain as usual."

Another letter, written in June, was missing its first page, but Mollie summarized the contents: Albert wrote about "an

Albert listening to his love letters read in court.

entertainment." In the rest of the letter, he said he hardly knew on which side his head stood. Albert said he would answer Mollie's letter and asked if he could call her his girl. He assured her he would never turn traitor. He did not enjoy Decoration Day (Memorial Day), as he had not made preparations, but he did go fishing in the morning. He told her not to be surprised to see him Saturday, as he was anxious to see her. He signed it "B.F."

On July 16, the same day Mrs. Little found Albert and Bessie in the barn together, Albert wrote another letter to Mollie. He opened the letter with "My Dear Friend" and wrote of the recent passing of his friend Olive Bock and being a pallbearer at her funeral. Albert mentioned his horse was sick and then wrote, "I'm anxious to have a good talk with you whether it be yay or nay. Will see you Saturday. Bert."

Albert's final letter to Mollie was dated August 27, the night Bessie died, and mailed the next day. The time written on the letter was 9:00 p.m. Albert told Mollie he was sorry she was sick and said he wouldn't laugh at her for being ill from overwork. He knew there was a lot of work to do on a farm and had no use for anyone who was too lazy to work. He said he believed in doing what the Bible said: "Thou shalt earn thy bread by the sweat of thy brow."

Albert said that if he thought Mollie to be crazy, she would have never found him in her presence. He regretted certain rumors she had heard, and he was sorry she said he needn't answer her anymore. She had heard he associated with "bad girls." Albert said he couldn't associate with her if he was intimate with bad women. He had reformed, he said, and was sorry she didn't believe it. He thought as much of her as he always had—and possibly more, if she was willing to cut ties with him over the rumors she heard. He called her a noble, true-hearted woman and told her he wanted to call on her to explain. Albert made a joke about seeing her other suitor and then closed the letter asking her to let him hear from her again, signed it "Bert." He then added, "P.S. I would much rather you would keep this letter under your own preservation, as this is between you and I."

This last letter created a sensation in the court. Kumler argued that this letter was written in cold blood after Bessie's murder. Albert then showed up at Reverend Teeter's home at 9:20 p.m. Kumler argued that Albert was able to compose himself enough to write the letter to Mollie before arriving at the Teeter house and falling into a swoon.

When the defense questioned Mollie, she admitted these were not all the letters Albert had written to her, but she did not know where the rest were. She was not sure how many times Albert called on her, but he was not her only suitor. She was also seeing a man named W.M. Kleppinger, who had called on her as many times as Albert. She had been trying to keep Albert hidden from Kleppinger. She last saw Albert on July 25 at a party she hosted.

Mrs. Little was recalled to the stand to confirm Bessie's age. Mrs. Little said when she got Bessie, she was one year old; she would have turned two the following year. She was pretty sure it was 1875 when Bessie came home with her. Bessie's name was originally Tress Doty.

Court adjourned for lunch, and Albert was escorted back to the jail. For comfort, Albert spent his time reading passages from the Bible his sister gave him and singing hymns. Other prisoners often joined him in singing some of his favorite songs, like "Home Over There" and "Nothing but the Blood of Jesus."

As Albert walked back to the courthouse, he glared at the massive crowd blocking the pathway. The lack of sleep and eating affected not only his appearance but his mood as well. Back in the courtroom, Albert's father, Jacob, was waiting for him. Jacob had not left Albert's side, attending court every day and sitting behind his son. The strain of the trial was wearing on him, but he was holding up well in spite of the stress. He walked with a cane and often took medicine for his illness.

After court resumed, Mr. Peter Little was called back to the stand. An attempt was made to establish Bessie's true age, but Mr. Little was unable to give information to clarify.

The books Albert read daily.

Mrs. Little was called back and asked about a letter from Bessie she was to bring to court. She'd brought the letter with her that day, and it was given to ex-prosecutor Patterson. After the prosecution turned the letter over to the defense to allow them to review it, the defense read the letter to the court.

The letter was dated August 10 and addressed to Bessie's "Dear Friends at Home." Bessie said in the letter that her parents had turned her out of the house. She was longing to see her friends at home, but since she was barred from returning to the house, she could only write to them. She hoped that "Bert" could persuade his father to allow him to marry her, because if he couldn't, she feared she would not be around much longer. Bessie asked for her clothes and said she'd call for them and pick them up outside the side door. If her parents wouldn't allow that, she'd send a boy to go get them.

Noah Brookins was recalled and asked again about the fire. Brookins said he saw the fire when it was first discovered and no one was there yet. He saw flames bursting from the side of the barn out of the south door, and he was sure nobody could have entered the barn without endangering their life.

The first witness for the defense was Mrs. Teeter, wife of Reverend Teeter. The Teeters had company for dinner the evening of August 27: two sisters who worked in the office of J.F. Cappel, where Reverend Teeter was also employed. After the company left, the Teeters were briefly alone at home before Albert called. Mrs. Teeter corroborated the story her husband told when he testified. The prosecution asked if Albert had any blood on his clothing when he called, and Mrs. Teeter said she did not remember seeing any.

Howard Hughes came to the stand and said he was the one to take the note from Bessie at the Hotel Cooper to Albert's father. He did not read the note, and he did not see Jacob Frantz read it either.

Jacob Frantz was then assisted to the witness stand to testify. A chair was put in front of the jury for him to sit, as he was unable to step up to the stand. Jacob was an invalid with iron-gray hair and a matching beard. Isaac was his oldest son, Albert his youngest. They had lived in the county for the past two years. Although Jacob knew Mr. Little and Bessie, he did not know Mrs. Little. Bessie once visited him at his home and asked if he intended to allow Albert to marry her. He told Bessie he did not and that he needed Albert at home to take care of him. Bessie visited a second time with the same question and threatened suicide if Albert did not marry her. Jacob described the letter he received from Mrs. Little, in which she said she was glad Bessie wasn't related to her and that she was from "low stock."

Jacob said the letter he received from Bessie while she was staying at the Hotel Cooper said she was sorry to bother an old man like him with his son's misdeeds, but she wanted Albert to right the wrong he had done her and marry her. If he didn't, she threatened to take her life and get the family into trouble. Bessie told Jacob about the night Albert left his shoes at her home and where he could get them. Jacob showed the letter from Bessie to Albert, who claimed he was only paying her board because she was homeless. Jacob claimed to not know anything about a pregnancy.

Jacob then said that on the night of the fire, Albert was in the house writing a letter. Jacob also said Albert was home the night Bessie was murdered until after supper. He did not know where Albert went after that. He had first heard of the murder in the newspaper.

Jacob Frantz, Isaac Frantz's father.

When cross-examined, Jacob told the prosecution he was up the night of August 27 when Albert came home. Jacob said he spoke with Albert and saw nothing unusual in his conduct. Jacob then went to bed at nine o'clock; Albert and Mattie stayed up. Jacob remembered his son Isaac came to visit the next day, and Isaac and Albert went out to the yard to talk after supper.

Jacob claimed he was the first one to discover the fire. He told Albert to get the horse and buggy out of the barn, and Albert ran out to the yard. He returned moments later to get a large knife from the kitchen to cut the horse's halter. Jacob then called after his son to tell him not to go into the stable or he'd burn up.

Jacob was seventy-three and had a spinal disease; he said Albert often helped him to bed at night. Albert also helped him walk. His son was a good lad who went to Sabbath school and never smoked or chewed.

Elsie Baker, who attended United Brethren Sunday School with Bessie, was called to identify her handwriting. She was shown a letter Bessie had allegedly written and confirmed the handwriting to be Bessie's.

John Mathias, president and general manager of Mathias Planing Mill, attended the Home Avenue United Brethren Church with Albert and thought his reputation was good. He knew Albert to be a peaceable and quiet man who attended church regularly with Bessie. Albert had worked for the company for eighteen months. Mathias had also received a letter from Bessie, which was written from the Hotel Cooper on August 17. In the letter, Bessie said she was homeless and friendless. She confessed that some of the rumors about her and Albert were true and she wanted him to marry her as soon as possible. She feared Mr. Regan was trying to make Albert lose his job by telling more than what was true of him. She feared this would work him harm, and she hoped Regan wouldn't negatively influence Mathias the way he'd influenced her parents about Albert. Regan was always watching her house, and she blamed him for most of the trouble for telling all he saw and heard. Her mother, Mrs. Little, had said some really cruel and hurtful things about her that she'd never forget. Bessie said she was all alone in the world and had to write to someone. Albert had been really good to her by getting her a place to stay, but she regretted that it was so expensive.

Maggie Mohlen was next to testify. She lived near the Little residence and once saw Albert and Bessie together. Bessie was crying, and Albert was trying to comfort her. Maggie heard Albert say something to the effect of, "You go, and I will take care of you."

Dr. A.E. Jenner had been practicing medicine for nearly fifty years. He served as a surgeon with the Fifth Ohio for three years. When asked about bullets being fired into the head near the bony part of the skull near the ear, he said there'd be difficulty in a suicide doing so, depending on the explosion. At the least, it would probably produce a concussion. He said a person working themselves up to do a thing like suicide could potentially shoot themselves twice. He said this was improbable, but it was possible. He added that the impact of the first shot would likely change the position of the second shot.

In demonstration, defense attorney Nevin pointed a revolver at his own head while questioning Dr. Jenner. Ex-prosecutor Patterson piped up that he'd better verify the gun wasn't loaded. When Nevin made a smart remark about taking his chances, Judge Brown said the court didn't want to take a chance. Prosecutor Kumler mentioned the case of Clement Vallandigham, the lawyer who accidentally shot himself while defending a client. Chief Farrell examined the revolver and determined it to be unloaded.

The defense then recalled Dr. O.E. Francis. Dr. Francis believed it was possible for a person to fire two shots into their own head, especially if the muzzle was stuck in their ear, but the position of the gun would change from the first to the second shot due to the force of the explosion.

Dr. King, former superintendent of the Dayton Insane Asylum, was called next. As a doctor, his expertise was requested to answer whether Bessie could have shot herself twice in the ear. Dr. King said if the muzzle of the revolver was lodged in the ear, he believed it would be impossible to fire a second shot after the first was fired.

Court was adjourned until the next morning.

Chapter 10

THE TRIAL: THE STUDEBAKER DEFENSE

Wednesday, December 23, 1896

Court proceedings began late the morning of December 23. During the wait, several men were kicked out for spitting on the floor. Albert looked exhausted; the sleepless nights were catching up to him. He barely spoke to anyone, giving a short greeting to his family and friends who showed up to support him.

The jury had a better night than Albert. Juror Isaac Haynes had a restless and talkative night, wrestling with his mules in his sleep. He yelled for "Bill" repeatedly, then had a long talk with someone who made him laugh loudly several times. He called for Bill again and then started to cry. The other jurors had a good laugh at the entertainment.

First to the stand, Jacob Frantz stated he needed to amend his testimony. Jacob said he did not see his son on the day of the murder after he returned from his drive—in fact, he did not see him until the next day at noon. Jacob claimed he'd just been confused.

Zenas Craig of Craig Reynolds Foundry Company saw the barn fire and thought nothing suspicious of it. He thought the blaze was too hot to risk his life to save the horse. His statement was ruled out because it was his opinion and did not provide objective facts about the case.

Dr. King, former superintendent of the Dayton Insane Asylum, resumed the stand and said he believed it would be impossible for a suicide to fire a second shot into their ear as described. If the gun was held away from the ear, he thought it might be possible to fire a second shot, but he didn't care to measure the chances of that happening.

Mrs. Isabel Fowler met Bessie at the Hotel Cooper. Bessie called on her often, and they spoke about Albert. Bessie said if Albert didn't marry her, she would take her own life. Another time, Bessie called on Mrs. Fowler and simply cried the entire visit. When she moved to the next boardinghouse, Bessie called again, hoping Mrs. Fowler would be her roommate, but Mrs. Fowler could not do so. Bessie again hinted at suicide and said goodbye. Mrs. Fowler encouraged Bessie to go home, but she said she could only do that if she gave up on Albert, and she wouldn't.

Scott McDonald used to be the proprietor of a gun store and sold firearms. He was shown a gun similar to the one Albert purchased and asked if all revolvers required the same finger strength to pull the trigger. McDonald said it depended on the spring and that some revolvers are easier to explode than the one he held.

Jesse Kumler lived near the Frantz family, saw the fire at the barn and was among the first to reach the scene. When describing the scene, Kumler said when the barn door was opened, flames burst out from the barn. He asked Albert for a crowbar or an ax, and Albert said there was nothing like that around the house.

Mrs. Brookins lived next door, and by the time she saw the stable fire, the entire interior was in flames. Albert kept his ax in his barn, she said. The next day, he came to her to borrow an ax.

Arthur Koogle was next to testify. A wagonmaker by trade, he was enlisted by the defense to buy a revolver from Dodd's Gun Store on December 11. Poince, the gun store clerk, testified he could identify anyone who bought a revolver from him, including Albert. When asked to identify a customer who bought a revolver from him recently, Poince was unable to identify Koogle in court.

When cross-examined, Koogle said Judge Kreitzer gave him $5.00 and sent him to the store. The revolver cost $3.50.

Patterson questioned him: "When you went into the gun store, didn't you have your coat collar turned up, your hat pulled down over your eyes, and keep your face turned away?"

"Why yes, I had my coat buttoned up," replied Koogle.

"When you were in this courtroom, didn't you turn your face away every time he looked in your direction?" asked Patterson.

When Koogle hesitated to answer, Patterson shouted at him. "Tell me, speak out!" he cried.

How Colonel Nevin told Koogle to disguise himself when buying the revolver.

Koogle then admitted that he did not want Poince to recognize him in court. He also admitted he was not wearing the same coat or hat the day Poince was asked to recognize him in the courtroom.

J.C. Bond, an out-of-town telephone operator, knew Albert and Bessie. He vouched for Albert's character and said Bessie was robust and stout, well-proportioned and weighed 140 to 145 pounds.

Margaret and Jeanette Chalmers were out on the bridge the evening of August 27. Both heard a shot near the Athletic Park, which is next to the bridge. They fixed the time after 7:00 p.m.

ALBERT'S REPUTATION

Several witnesses were called to testify to Albert's character and reputation.

John R. Miller, a schoolteacher living west of the city, knew Albert to be a quiet, peaceable young man.

Elsie Baker, a young lady acquaintance, had known Albert since the previous winter. Albert called on her a few times, but she did not consider him regular company. They went buggy riding once.

Byron Weldy of West Charleston said he'd known Albert for fifteen years and knew him to be peaceable and quiet. When cross-examined, he admitted he'd lived in Toledo for the fifteen years he knew Albert and had not interacted with Albert since he moved to Dayton.

W.H. Kleppinger said he was a friend of Albert's and thought him to be peaceable and quiet.

S.R. Fergus, a Miami County justice of the peace, knew Albert before he moved to Dayton. He thought him to be a peaceable and quiet guy. When cross-examined, he admitted to knowing Albert only when he was sixteen or seventeen and that he knew nothing of his reputation since.

W.H. Dietrick, trustee of Columbia Township, declared Albert a well-behaved young man with a good reputation. Under cross-examination, he said he knew nothing of Albert in the last few years.

W.D. Long, a Dunkard dentist, knew Albert for seven or eight years and said he had a good reputation.

W.H. and Clarence Deam of West Charleston testified to Albert's good reputation as well. Both stated they hadn't seen much of Albert in the previous six years.

Reverend O.P. Hoover, a Dunkard minister, thought Albert's reputation to be good. He knew of Albert calling on some young ladies.

Cornelius Bone, superintendent of the Miami County Infirmary, brought the record of a woman named Edith Doty. Edith was admitted on September 11, 1871, with her daughter Tress (Bessie). She was an alcoholic and unable to care for herself or her child. The child's father was unknown. The child was taken home by the Littles on October 28, 1871. This proved Bessie was older than previously realized, putting her age closer to twenty-five or twenty-six.

Albert's defense primarily centered on two main points. One: Bessie committed suicide by shooting herself twice in the head. Two: when Albert dumped Bessie's body, it was due to temporary insanity inherited from his mother's side of the family.

To demonstrate that Bessie was in the state of mind to kill herself, the defense pointed to the behavior she exhibited at the Hotel Cooper. Bessie believed she was pregnant, and her anxiety increased as the days passed. The longer Albert delayed marriage, the more likely others would notice signs of pregnancy and her reputation would be ruined. During her time at the Hotel Cooper, Bessie befriended Mrs. Amanda Bell, bookkeeper. Bessie confided in Mrs. Bell, telling her often of her concerns about Albert.

Bessie had told several of her friends that she believed Albert was deceiving her and she feared going buggy riding with him because he had recently been carrying a revolver. Bessie was also known to have fits of despondency. One night a few weeks before her death, she was out with a friend, and they were crossing the Third Street bridge over the Miami River. The river was very high that day. Bessie stopped, looked over the water and said she had a notion to jump in and drown herself. Her friend persuaded her not to do so.

THE CRAZY STUDEBAKERS

During Colonel Nevin's statement to the court, he addressed the fact that Albert was a Studebaker by blood on his mother's side. Colonel Nevin asserted that Albert's behavior was due in part to having Studebaker blood flowing through his veins. Many of the witnesses to the Studebakers' odd behavior were their neighbors from Indiana, outside of the court's jurisdiction. This fact left the court with no authority to compel the witnesses to testify. To get their statements, the defense went to Indiana to gather depositions to establish the "insane" reputation of the Studebaker family.

The depositions came from neighbors and physicians who had encountered members of the Studebaker family, along with two Studebakers who were considered to be sane. The witnesses questioned were Artemas Smith, Isaac Studebaker, William Mason, Dr. William Loop, Lewis Kuszmaul, David Studebaker and Dr. Joseph Rogers. Through their depositions, the defense was able to paint a picture of the members of the Studebaker family in question:

ABRAHAM STUDEBAKER: Albert's grandfather. Abraham was not known to be insane but considered "too nice to poor people."

PHOEBE STUDEBAKER: Albert's mother, considered not to be insane. She died of cancer around 1890. As far as witnesses knew, neither she nor her children ever had mental health issues.

Phoebe's siblings:
REBECCA (STUDEBAKER) NEHER: Rebecca, Phoebe's twin sister, had been "insane" for fourteen years and was confined to the insane asylum in Dayton. Her record from the Dayton Asylum read, "Admitted July 13, 1896, age 65. Has three insane brothers, was admitted to insane asylum once previously; insanity hereditary, homicidal, not suicidal."

ABRAM STUDEBAKER: Abram was committed to the Dayton asylum in 1886. His record read, "Age 62, admitted September 8, 1886, married, from Miami County, religion German Baptist. Homicidal, but not suicidal, insanity hereditary. Has been admitted to asylums four times previously."

JOSEPH STUDEBAKER: Joseph was known to have had some spells of epilepsy, which made others consider him insane in the 1890s.

JOHN STEELE STUDEBAKER: John had been committed to an asylum in Indianapolis roughly twenty-five years prior for a seven-week period and was later confined to an asylum near Logansport, Indiana, for a period of two years. John had four children who committed suicide and another who had attempted but was rescued in time. John was described as sharp and sane except when it came to family dealings. He was known to be abusive to his children. He suffered from "spells" of insanity, along with delusions of grandeur and bouts of paranoia. At the time of the trial, John S. was under the care of a guardian.

John had intended to give each of his sons $600 when they turned twenty-one to get them started in adulthood. To aid in this effort, John split some of his land into smaller lots and sold them off. Unfortunately for the younger sons, John was unable to pay up once they came of age. Not only was he unable to give them the money, but he also did not have land to provide for them. Two of the younger sons, Amos and Daniel, even had to bail their father out during financial troubles, leading to family arguments.

John's children, Albert's first cousins:
GEORGE STUDEBAKER, TWENTY-TWO: George was described as a bright boy who studied at the Terre Haute Normal School and excelled in math. Not

getting the inheritance money from his father caused a rift between George and John. After an argument between the two, John left the house to go to town, but before he got there, he received word that George had killed himself. Shortly after the argument, George had gone to an upstairs room in the house and shot himself twice, once in the chest and once in the head.

Daniel Studebaker, twenty-eight: Shortly after Daniel came of age, he realized he would not be receiving the money he expected from his father, causing multiple arguments between father and son. Daniel hanged himself in the family barn.

Barbara (Studebaker) Harless, fifty-two: Barbara married and moved from Indiana to Nebraska. She died from self-administered poison.

John Studebaker Jr.: John Jr. was described as having a bad temperament when he was young, but he didn't show signs of insanity until around age thirty-five. He served in the military with his brother David. John Jr. got into an argument with his neighbor over some hay and accused him of setting fires on his land. He told his family physician, Dr. Loop, about the argument. When he didn't get the reaction he wanted, he threatened Dr. Loop with

The sons of John S. Studebaker. *Front row, left to right*: David, John, Isaac, Jacob. *Back row*: George, Daniel, Amos, Joseph.

a knife. Dr. Loop told him to get out of his office, and John Jr. complied. He returned later with a gun and threatened Dr. Loop again. Unruffled, Dr. Loop told him to leave and not come back. John left the physician's office, went first to his neighborhood and then to the home of his neighbor, opened the door to his house and fired. He was tried for murder and pleaded not guilty due to insanity. He was then committed to an insane asylum in Topeka, Kansas. He was considered the most violent and dangerous patient in the institution.

JACOB STUDEBAKER, FORTY: Jacob had been committed to an asylum for paranoia and delusions. When he was first admitted to the hospital, he was very agitated and believed his brothers were conspiring to kill him and steal his land. (As one of John S.'s older sons, Jacob had received money and property from his father when he came of age. He believed his younger brothers who had not received money or land were conspiring against him.) Jacob also believed he was being pursued by White Caps, a vigilante group in Southern Indiana known for enforcing its moral codes, often by lynching. After treatment in the asylum, Jacob showed improvement and, when released, moved to Nebraska and married. His mental health later regressed, and he shot himself.

AMOS STUDEBAKER: Although Amos attempted suicide, he was not successful. He stepped up onto a buggy and hanged himself. His wife, suspecting what he was about to do, ran to the neighbors for help. They arrived in time to cut him down and save his life. Later, Amos told his brother Isaac that he just couldn't see his way any further and thought the only option was suicide. Amos was deeply in debt and having marital problems. After the attempt, Amos reconciled with his wife.

David Studebaker, one of the oldest of John S. Studebaker's living sons, remarked that their mother, Elizabeth Landis, came from a family with a history of contrariness. When questioned about two of his uncles on his mother's side who had exhibited odd behavior, he remarked that their behavior was due to contrariness, not insanity.

Throughout the depositions, David and Isaac Studebaker both said they met Albert years before when he was a boy and they knew nothing of him as an adult.

After the depositions were read, Miss Mattie Frantz, Albert's sister, took the stand. She testified that her mother had been dead eight years and she was responsible for Albert. While he was a minor, Mattie was in charge of Albert's estate until he came of age, which was the previous November 24. Since Albert was in jail, no settlement had been reached for his $1,700 inheritance.

Mattie knew Bessie and believed Albert loved her and wanted to marry her, but both Mattie and their father objected to the marriage. She claimed not to know of Albert's secret visits to Bessie at night and not to know where his shoes were. Mattie read the letter Bessie sent to her father from the Hotel Cooper and burned it. Mattie claimed in the letter that Bessie said, "If Bert does not marry me I will make it cost your family sweetly. It will not cost me anything to take my life."

Mattie Frantz, Albert's sister.

Mattie burned the letter Mrs. Little wrote to Jacob as well. When asked why she burned them, she said she didn't want them to upset her father.

Mattie was home the night of the fire. Her father opened the parlor door, and they discovered the flames. She and Albert ran to the fire, and Mattie told her brother he wouldn't be able to rescue the horse. Mattie had also been home the previous night: she had supper with Albert around six o'clock, then he left in the buggy. She didn't see him again until the next morning, when he was getting ready for work. He did not eat anything for breakfast, saying he wasn't hungry. He barely ate dinner and supper that day too.

Mattie once asked Albert why he was paying board for Bessie, and he said, "I pity her, she has no home." Mattie knew Albert was seeing other girls but did not know how many.

Before closing out the day, the defense recalled Cassius Bond. Previously, Bond had referred to Bessie as "strong and stout," and the state was hoping he could explain that statement a bit more. Bond told the story of a country party where he and Bessie played Old Dan Tucker, a dance where they would swing each other by the hands. It was then he noticed Bessie was unusually strong. Patterson laughingly dismissed the witness with no more questions.

Chapter 11

THE TRIAL: CHRISTMAS BREAK

THURSDAY, DECEMBER 24, 1896

Court started late again, and Albert looked the worse for wear. The ladies showed up in full force, the majority having not missed a day since the trial started. Albert showed no interest in them, looking the other way when he walked past.

The defense started the day by finishing reading the depositions left over from the previous day. When they were done, Albert's lawyers took him into another room for a consultation, and when they came back out, Albert looked sullen and a bit paler than usual. During the consultation, Albert had requested not to take the stand. At this point, Colonel Nevin announced that the defense's legal battle had concluded.

After this announcement, the state asked to recall several witnesses to be called in rebuttal. The State left the room to consult with the witnesses, then returned.

First called was bailiff Boes, who testified he saw Arthur Koogle turn his head when Poince was looking around the courtroom to identify him. Boes stood with his head turned away from the witness stand to show how Koogle stood.

W.L. Bloomer and Ed Anthony, artists of the *Cincinnati Post*, had sketched Koogle and noticed he turned his face away from Poince.

Salesman Poince was then recalled. He stated Koogle called at Dodd's Gun Store one evening after the lamps outside had ignited. Koogle wore a dark overcoat with the collar turned up and a slouch hat pulled down over his face. Colonel Nevin fixed his collar up, pulled his hat down over his face and made a show of telling the jury that if he were dressed like that, nobody would sell him a gun.

After Poince, the state also rested. Since it was Christmas Eve, the court released all witnesses and adjourned for the day. Both sides agreed to wait until Monday (December 28) to start again.

FRIDAY, DECEMBER 25, 1896

To celebrate the Christmas holiday, special meals were prepared for the prisoners. For dinner, they were served escalloped oysters, mashed potatoes, coleslaw, celery, bread, butter, fruit and cigars. For supper, they had bread and butter, coffee, crullers and oranges. Albert still didn't have a good appetite and ate sparingly of the meals offered. He spent Christmas morning in his cell reading his Bible and devotions. He was even inspired at one point to tell a story about Jesus and Christmas.

Albert spent most of his time in deep thought, the weight of the trial on his shoulders. Sometimes he'd speak about religion with his fellow prisoners, but when he returned to his cell after court on Christmas Eve, he remained quiet, hardly speaking at all.

Albert's mood brightened a bit when talk of a traveling man who'd wrestled a gun away from Bessie began circulating. Allegedly, a traveling man had stopped at the Hotel Cooper and persuaded Bessie to give the gun to him instead of using it to shoot herself. When the investigation into Bessie's death started, a look into the story turned up no such traveling man to corroborate it.

During Christmas week, a letter received by Albert's attorneys introduced the story of a traveling drug salesman from northern Ohio who claimed to have taken a gun from Bessie at the Hotel Cooper while she was boarding there. They sent for the traveling salesman upon receiving the letter, and he was expected to arrive in Dayton on Christmas evening.

The jurors had a lonely Christmas. Since they weren't allowed to return home to their families, they spent the day in the charge of bailiff Boes.

Sunday, December 27, 1896

The jury attended church at First Reform, where Reverend William Hale preached an eloquent Christmas sermon. Judge Brown and bailiff Boes then took the jury to the National Soldiers Home, where they took a tour. Afterward, they were escorted to Huffman's Hill.

Several of the jurors had been sick over the weekend, warranting three physicians to attend to them over the Christmas weekend. By Sunday, they were all feeling much better, and there was no concern for the trial that day.

For the first time in a long time, Albert was in a cheerful mood—perhaps it was the break from the trial or the Christmas celebrations or maybe even just being able to relax. Regardless, Albert was in high spirits. He spent most of that Sunday reading devotionals and singing hymns.

Albert's voice rang out through the old stone corridors of the "castle of sighs." He read the newspapers, showing intense interest in the events and happenings of the city. His appetite was hearty, and he ate his full dinner for the first time since the trial began. It seemed as if Albert thought this affair was soon to be over.

If his high spirits were due to the talk of Bessie obtaining a revolver, they were soon to be dashed. Once Chief Farrell heard of the traveling salesman rumor, he immediately went to work investigating the story. It did not take him long to find that the Bessie in the story was not Bessie Little. By coincidence, it was another woman named Bessie, and this incident took place a month after Bessie Little died.

This Bessie had procured a revolver, and on learning she intended to kill herself, the traveling salesman convinced her to give it up. This event did not take place at the Hotel Cooper and had nothing to do with Bessie Little. After giving up her revolver, Chief Farrell learned, the other Bessie attempted to purchase morphine for the same cause.

Chapter 12

THE TRIAL: CLOSING ARGUMENTS

Monday, December 28, 1896

The largest crowd of the entire trial had formed outside the courtroom in hopes of getting a seat inside to hear the closing arguments. The size and excitement of the crowd warranted an extra guard present to escort Albert into the building. Despite his feeling cheerful and well-rested the day before, Albert's eyes were red and swollen, and it was clear he had not slept well the previous night. His countenance was pale, and he was visibly nervous.

Once Albert had taken his seat, his sister Mattie rushed to his side and kissed him. His brother Isaac and their father clasped his hands warmly, as if transferring their strength to him. The rest of his relatives were in attendance, weeping intermittently, anxious for the day's proceedings.

PROSECUTION

Former prosecutor J.C. Patterson opened with a tale of a young woman lured to the Stillwater Bridge by a man she trusted, who then murdered her and threw her body into the river. Bessie had threatened to press charges against Albert but dropped them when he sweet-talked her, proving Albert's motive to kill her.. Albert had the threat of charges hanging over his head unless he married Bessie. Surgical science, Patterson declared, proved beyond a doubt that Bessie, unfamiliar with firearms, couldn't have shot herself twice in the

Colonel Patterson.

manner described. Patterson not only argued that it wasn't possible but also asked: If she really had done so, how could an honorable lover have just discarded her body into the "swift current of the merciless river" and, instead of getting her help, gone home and written a letter implying a proposal to another woman? Albert was guilty of murder in the first degree, he argued, and he planned Bessie's death with malice and premeditation.

Patterson referred to the defense's attempt to sabotage the witness identification of Arthur Koogle by salesclerk Poince in court, Koogle having turned his head away from Poince as he looked around the courtroom to identify his customer. He also pointed out that the defense had made no attempts to find out where Bessie had purchased a gun, as they claimed she had.

Patterson painted Albert as a cruel, cold-blooded lover who killed Bessie to avoid marriage. Albert had commented to one of his coworkers at the planing mill that he'd rather squander his inheritance from his mother's estate in litigation than be compelled to marry Bessie.

Another bit of evidence to bolster the prosecution's claim was Albert's fascination with the Pearl Bryan murder case from earlier that year. In February 1896, Pearl's headless body was found in northern Kentucky. She was five months pregnant. Pearl was unmarried and traveling with her lover and his friend. Her lover did not want to marry her or care for their child, so with the help of his friend, he murdered her in cold blood. Pearl's head was never found. Albert was fascinated with the case and studied every bit of information about it he could find, even visiting the crime scene several times. On his last visit, he commented to his friend that it was a botched job.

Miss Mollie Cart offered strong evidence that Albert did not intend to marry Bessie, as he had promised her several times. He had written to Mollie frequently since the previous March and had even proposed marriage. His last letter to her was dated August 27, the night Bessie died. With the blood of his slain lover saturating his clothes, he calmly penned Mollie a letter consisting of twelve closely written pages, referring to social functions they both attended and events to come. He closed the letter with a request that she keep it a secret between them. Before he finished writing the letter, his father walked through the room on his way to bed and fixed the hour at 9:00 p.m. Twenty minutes later, Albert appeared at the Teeter residence, dramatically declaring the suicide of Bessie Little before swooning on the couch.

In closing, Patterson asked the jury to deal with Albert as they would a "despoiler and murderer" of a wife or daughter in their own homes.

Defense

Colonel Nevin started the defense's closing statement with:

> *Gentleman of the jury: You promised all concerned that you would form no conclusions in this case until at the close of the arguments and the charge of His Honor you would return to the room provided for your deliberation, lock the doors behind you, and there consider in your own minds without passion, without prejudice, without the influence of assumed logic or of brilliant eloquence, the problem which you have been called to solve.*

Nevin laid out the difference between first degree and second degree murder, harping especially on the fact that first degree murder requires malice and premeditation. As Nevin broke apart the pieces of the crime, it became evident he was trying to introduce the jury to the idea of a second degree murder verdict instead, which would spare Albert's life.

Nevin traced Bessie's history, noting she had been a "waif" or abandoned child, and as a result, it could not be determined that she had not inherited suicidal tendencies from her bloodline. Nevin declared Bessie died brokenhearted by the vicious gossip circulating among her neighbors and friends, along with the hateful words spoken by her foster mother, Mrs. Little. Since Bessie believed she was pregnant, her anxiety increased with every day that passed, her fear of being exposed intensifying. She was in such a state

Colonel Nevin.

of mind that she must have ended her own life. Additionally, Nevin argued, there was no proof Albert ever planned to kill his sweetheart.

Nevin excused Albert's hesitation to marry Bessie, citing the age difference between them. Bessie had been legally mature for several years, whereas Albert was still not legally mature at the time of her death. Because of this, Albert was not able to marry her without his father's permission, which he did not have.

Raising his voice to a thunderous pitch, Nevin declared that no matter the outcome of the trial, the time would come when it was revealed that Albert never bought a revolver from Dodd's Gun Store. Furthermore, he must have been either the greatest actor ever or genuinely upset when he arrived at the Teeters' home, prostrate with grief, and swooned on their chair. Nevin said the very act of throwing Bessie into the water was proof he was innocent, as the water was so deep and the current so strong that Albert could have thrown her in and killed her without shooting her.

Colonel Nevin concluded his speech by asking the jury to restore the son of Old Man Frantz to him as a Christmas present. At his plea, Albert began to cry, wiping away his tears with a handkerchief.

Judge Kreitzer was the next speaker. Albert's greatest mistake, he announced, was dumping Bessie's body into the river instead of bringing her back to the city and to the police.

Kreitzer questioned Mollie Cart's assertion that Albert was her "regular company," noting she also kept company with a man named Kleppinger and he was the object of her affection. Kreitzer argued that John Herby and his daughter could not have heard a scream at the bridge before shots were fired simply because their home was too far away. If Bessie were alive, he said she'd have this to say: "Spare that young man's life. He is innocent of my blood. I took my life because I was tired of living. Driven from home and despondent in my sin and misfortune, I sought relief in death."

Giving the last statement for the defense's closing argument was W.H. Van Skaik. To answer the question of why Bessie didn't take her life in a more public place, he cited a letter Bessie wrote to Albert's father before her death. In it, she threatened to take her life at the expense of the Frantz family. It was unlikely she screamed before shooting herself, he said. But if she did, it was part of her scheme. "Gentleman of the jury," he declared. "We have shown that Bessie Little repeatedly declared she intended to take her life."

Regarding the letter Albert wrote to Mollie Cart, Van Skaik declared he must have written the letter at a different time and simply dated it 9:00 p.m. on August 27 to establish an alibi.

Finding a stopping point, court adjourned for the day.

Chapter 13

THE TRIAL: VERDICT

TUESDAY, DECEMBER 29, 1896

The last day of Albert's trial was a dreary, rainy one. The weather dampened not only the streets but also the excitement of the crowd gathering outside the courtroom. The courtroom inside the building was filled; the ladies were in full attendance as usual. Albert had had a restless night and skipped breakfast, his nerves too on edge to function normally. The jury had a good night, but bailiff Boes did not. He had a severe attack of neuralgia and suffered greatly.

By 9:30, the weather had cleared, and the crowd poured in. They forced their way into the building, and it became nearly impossible to come or go from the courtroom.

Before Van Skaik could resume his closing statement, Chief Farrell presented evidence regarding the story of Bessie buying a revolver with intent to end her own life. In Judge Brown's private room, Chief Farrell presented Mrs. Bessie Bennett, the young woman in question. When she was questioned on the matter, Bessie Bennett made a statement:

> *Some months before my marriage I was in the company with a traveling man. I owned a revolver and happened to show it to him. He endeavored to take it away from me and we had a playful scuffle. I became somewhat alarmed that the weapon would be discharged and after that determined to dispose of it. A few days later I sold it at Lindsey's Gun Store. I had*

no intention of committing suicide but the traveling man joked me to that effect and said he intended to take the pistol away so that I could not kill myself. It has also been told that I attempted to buy morphine, after being deprived of the pistol. The fact seems to be that the traveling man has been talking very wide of the mark, but that there are some circumstances which seem to substantiate his story. Soon after I saw him, I did go to a drugstore at which he sells goods and endeavored to buy some morphine. I had no intention, however, of using it to kill myself, but wanted it simply to take for medicinal purposes. I am the Bessie in the case so far as the traveling man is concerned and am not afraid to go upon the witness stand and tell all about the matter.

Chief Farrell then took Mrs. Bennett to the courtroom, where she repeated her statement to the court and attorneys. As a result, the defense dropped the plan to indicate Bessie Little had a revolver and planned suicide with it. J.H. Tyler was the traveling man; he worked for Gall Drughouse of Kalamazoo, Michigan. His friends alleged that either Tyler confused Bessie Bennett and Bessie Little or Albert's attorneys misled Tyler so they could use him to benefit Albert's defense.

Van Skaik then resumed his argument, claiming Bessie committed suicide. He took apart the state's evidence piece by piece, harping on the fact that Bessie had threatened suicide several times over a few months prior to her death.

Court recessed for five minutes after Van Skaik concluded his speech.

When court resumed, a deep silence fell over the courtroom, making for a dramatic scene as Prosecutor Kumler arose to deliver his speech. As he made the closing argument, he picked apart the theory that Bessie committed suicide and destroyed many other statements made by the defense. Albert sank lower into his chair as he heard his story taken apart.

When Kumler concluded, Judge Brown addressed the jury and explained the charges they were to consider. He set out the indictment, made clear the law regarding the three different degrees of murder, then explained reasonable doubt. He said in order to find the defendant guilty of any degree of the crime, they must find him guilty of every essential ingredient that makes up the degree. He advised the jury to carefully weigh the evidence of the bullets and the testimony about whether a person could fire two shots into their own head and to consider the testimony about whether Bessie committed suicide. If the jury found that Bessie suicided, he said, then they need go no further.

Judge Brown told the jurors to consider carefully whether they believed Albert to be sane or insane at the time of Bessie's death. Judge Brown explained that the defense did not claim that Albert was insane at the time of trial but that his acts at the time of Bessie's death were not consistent with those of a sane person. The true test of responsibility when insanity is claimed, Judge Brown explained, is whether the accused has sufficient use of his reason to understand the motive of the act with which he is charged. If he did understand it, he was criminally responsible; if not, he was entitled to acquittal.

Judge Brown then explained in thorough detail the aspects of the six choices the jury could make regarding Albert Frantz: first degree murder, second degree murder, third degree murder, assault, assault and battery and acquittal. He then explained the concept of reasonable doubt and that the jurors must decide Albert's guilt beyond reasonable doubt or acquit.

Before dismissing the jurors to their room to deliberate, Judge Brown told them they'd be kept together in the charge of an officer until they agreed on a verdict or were discharged by the court.

Just before 3:00 p.m., the jury was escorted to the third floor of the courthouse, over Judge Brown's courtroom. It was a large, airy, well-ventilated room reached by a winding stairway. Once settled, they elected George Davis as jury foreman.

An hour later, the jury bell rang in the courtroom. A hush fell immediately on the court. Bailiff Boes went up to the jury room and returned minutes later, smiling. The jury just wanted a pitcher of water. The spectators and court personnel resumed their talking and laughing, but there was one in the courtroom who did not participate. Albert sat solemnly at the table, his head resting in his right hand, his elbow on the table. He sat still, barely moving unless spoken to by his friends or family. His father, sister and two brothers, Cornelius and Reverend Isaac, were present. Albert's father asked for his crutches and proceeded to shuffle from the courtroom to the old law library. He walked the floor anxiously at a slow pace, waiting to learn his son's fate.

Judge Brown had retired to his chamber but hurriedly returned to the bench when he heard the first jury bell ring. The attorneys from both sides rushed in as well, but when they all found out the jury just wanted water, they again left the courtroom.

At exactly 5:19, after slightly more than two hours of deliberation, the jury bell rang again. Every voice was hushed, and Albert first jumped as if startled and then fell back into his seat, trembling slightly. This time, the jury had reached a verdict. Bailiff Boes unlocked the jury room and brought the

The jury room where Albert's fate was determined.

jurors down the stairs and into the courtroom. Once they were seated, Judge Brown asked, "Gentleman, have you agreed upon a verdict?"

"We have," answered foreman Davis.

A small slip of paper containing the few words that sealed Albert's fate was handed to bailiff Boes, who then turned it over to deputy clerk William Hoskot. Judge Brown then ordered Hoskot to read the verdict.

The verdict read as follows:

> *We the jury, upon the issues joined in this case, find the defendant Albert J Frantz, GUILTY of murder in the first degree in manner and form as he stands charged in the indictment.*
> *(Signed) George W Davis, Foreman*

All eyes turned to Albert as he sat frozen, not uttering a single sound. Some thought he had fainted sitting up, but this idea was dispelled when his arms suddenly dropped to his sides and his body appeared to deflate. The color drained from his face, and he trembled in his seat. His head fell forward, then he began to cry, weeping and wailing as only a man meeting his fate with the executioner would.

The attorneys for the defense asked that the roll of jurors be called and each one asked if the verdict read was his verdict. As deputy Hoskot called the roll, each juror answered, "That is my verdict."

At the last juror's answer, Reverend Isaac Frantz wrung his hands and began to weep. Albert's other brother Cornelius fell from his seat to his knees, overturning his chair. He then struggled to his feet, waved his arms wildly above his head and dropped to the floor with a groan. He was unconscious by the time sheriffs reached his side to help him. They attempted to raise him off the floor, but he would not rouse. Mattie had been crying since the verdict was read and only cried harder at the sight of her brother on the floor. She struggled to her feet, stretched her arms wide and cried out, "Oh! My God! My God!"

Albert's weeping and the cries of his family sent chills down the spine of witnesses nearby, and the grief displayed by each family member only intensified the grief the other members felt. Seeing the effect on Albert and wanting to restore order to the court, Judge Brown ordered Albert to be taken from the room. Albert could scarcely walk, and he required three deputies to support him out of the room. He staggered like a drunk, and his cries sounded above the excited reactions of the audience.

Albert and his family reacting to the verdict.

To clear the way for the removal of Albert and his family members, the spectators were forbidden to leave. Half a dozen strong men carried Cornelius to Judge Brown's office, where Dr. Weaver and Dr. W.B. Smith tended to him. Mattie had recovered enough to sit at her brother's bedside, and it took nearly thirty minutes to revive him. Once awake, Cornelius became delirious and was removed by ambulance to the hospital. Jacob, the aged father of them all, had not yet heard the verdict, as he was still in the law library.

In his cell, Albert threw himself onto his bed in a burst of grief. He was up late that night, wringing his hands and weeping as he paced back and forth in his cell, much like Bessie used to in her room at the boardinghouse.

Later, the members of the jury met and signed the following letter addressed to Judge Brown and bailiff Boes and requested its publication as a compliment to the two gentlemen for their kind treatment while being sequestered.

> *We, the jurors in the Frantz case, take great pleasure in kindly thanking Judge O.B. Brown and our very efficient court bailiff, J.F. Boes.*
> *Resolved, that we will always hold them in kind remembrance and high esteem.*

Respectfully,
J.U. Daugherty
J.U. Shively
D.F. Giddinger
I.C. Haynes
Adolph Geige
Martin H. Young
Andrew H. Baker
Levi W. Mease
Dietrich Von Engle
George W. Davis
John Moler
Elijah Coler

Although talk of appeals started immediately after the verdict was read, Chief Farrell wasn't worried. He released a statement regarding the letter written by the anonymous man claiming to have been under the bridge with a local lady at the time of Bessie's murder. Initially, he had dismissed the letter as a publicity ploy by a newspaper, but he had finally made contact with one of the witnesses. The information came too late for the trial, but Chief Farrell was ready if another trial took place.

According to the witness, a male and a female companion were meeting under the Stillwater Bridge, seated on a large rock. They heard a buggy approach, its occupants in the throes of a bitter quarrel. The buggy was moving slowly, the horse leisurely walking.

The sounds of the argument caught their attention, and they listened intently. They snuck out from under the bridge to get a look, and they saw a horrifying sight. Albert grabbed Bessie by the neck and drew a shining pistol from his coat. When she screamed, he placed his hand over her mouth, pushed the weapon against her head and fired two shots.

At the sound of the shots, the horse reared and attempted to run away. It took a few moments for Albert to get the horse back under control, then he drove the buggy back to the bridge, where he threw Bessie's crumpled body over the railing into the river. Then he cracked his whip and drove the buggy quickly away, vanishing into the night.

The couple froze in horror as they watched the body sink into the muddy water. It did not rise back to the surface. They left the spot as quickly as possible and, fearing exposure, kept this knowledge to themselves. They argued over what to do and, in the interest of justice, wrote the letter from Nashville.

The story came directly from the female witness present that night. She had hesitated so long to come forward because her identity and hidden position at the bridge that night would have caused a lot of trouble and embarrassment for her. She held back to protect her good name but eventually could not keep quiet anymore. Chief Farrell kept their names secret but verified their story.

Chief Farrell also spoke out about coroner Corbin, accusing him of wanting to dismiss Bessie's death as a suicide and investigate no further.

> *I want to say that, while Coroner Corbin may have possessed certain information, he displayed no disposition to use it. On the contrary, that body would have lain buried in a pauper's grave as a suicide but for my demanding that it be taken up again. The coroner had decided it to be a suicide and was about to render his verdict accordingly. The body was taken up as I requested, that very night, and when brought to the city an examination was made in the presence of the Drs. Weaver, father and son, Dr. Crisman, the coroner and another physician, whose name has heretofore not been mentioned in the case. An examination of the head revealed the bullet wounds. The head was severed from the body and ordered by the coroner to be buried again. Dr. Bonner (formerly of Xenia) was the fourth physician. He requested that he be permitted to make a more thorough examination stating that he would do so for nothing. The coroner, however, declared that the body was too stinking and ordered it hurried away.*

When asked why the physicians pursued the course they did, Chief Farrell said it puzzled him. He could only suppose they wanted to dispose of the body as soon as possible since it was badly decomposed and offensive to handle.

After making this statement, Chief Farrell received a letter:

> *T.J. Farrell, Chief of Police:*
> *Sir—As sure as Albert J Frantz is executed, just so sure will your life and that of George W. Davis be forfeited. —C.M.*

Chapter 14

APPEALS

lbert's attorneys wasted no time in filing for an appeal in his case. Judge Kreitzer told a *Dayton Herald* reporter that there were several technical reasons for doing so and he thought the motion would be granted. When he filed the motion for a new trial in the Clerk of Courts Office, he gave ten reasons why a new trial should be granted. Here are the reasons as listed in the *Dayton Herald*:

> *First: Because there was error in the admission of certain testimony on behalf of the State, against the objection of this defendant.*
>
> *Second: Because there was error in the refusal of the court to admit certain testimony offered by the defendant.*
>
> *Third: Because of error in the charge of the court as given to the jury, to which defendant at the time excepted.*
>
> *Fourth: Because of misconduct on the part of the jury, in that certain of said jurors had formed and expressed an opinion as to the guilt of this defendant before they were sworn in said case.*
>
> *Fifth: Because of the misconduct of the jury, in that certain communications were made to said jury prejudicial to the defendant before they retired to the jury room, which communications were not offered in evidence in said case.*
>
> *Sixth: Because of newly discovered evidence since the trial and which this defendant and his counsel could not have discovered by the exercise of due diligence.*

Seventh: Because the verdict of the jury is contrary to the law of the case.

Eighth: Because the verdict of the jury is against the manifest weight of the evidence.

Ninth: Because the verdict of this case ought to have been for the defendant, apparent upon the fact of the record.

Tenth: Because of other errors, to the prejudice of this defendant, apparent upon the face of the record.

The motion was signed by Kreitzer & Kreitzer, W.H. Van Skaik and R.M. Nevin, the attorneys for the defendant.

Perhaps driven by hope of a new trial, Albert's appetite had returned, and he was able to eat a hearty breakfast. He'd been feeling low the previous day but felt better after a visit from his brother Isaac, his sister Mattie and other sister, Mrs. Wayne Pfouz, and his cousin Mrs. Teeter. Cornelius, Albert's brother who was removed from the court after a swoon, was taken to the home of his wife's family to recover fully. Albert occupied a single cell but had two roommates just the day before. Now the daytime guard, Phillip Marquardt, and the night guard, Edward Winters, were his sole companions.

Two weeks later, Albert's attorneys released another statement, giving more detail.

In the Common Pleas Court of Montgomery County, Ohio

State of Ohio vs. Albert Frantz

To the Hon. Charles H. Kumler and John C. Patterson, attorneys for the state:

Gentleman—as to that part of our motion for a new trial herein, which related to matters conducted by the jurors during this case, we expect to show that at or about the time efforts were being made to recover the pistol thrown into the river at the Stillwater Bridge, near Athletic Park, that one of the said jurors, Dietrich Von Engle, said substantially that Frantz was guilty, that it was a clear case against him, and that he believed or was satisfied that Frantz had killed the girl.

We expect to show that another of said jurors, Joseph Daugherty, was down at or near the bridge where the divers and others were at work searching for the pistol that was thrown into the river, and that while there he said substantially that Frantz was guilty.

As to another of said jurors, foreman of said jury, George Davis, we expect to show that about or near the same time as above indicated that he said that defendant Frantz was guilty of killing the girl, and that he ought to be hung.

We have learned that another juror had formed and expressed opinion as to the guilt of the defendant, but we have yet had no time to investigate it, and do not know whether it is true or not. We do not care to give the juror's name because if it is not true, he ought not to be prejudiced by any statement. If it is true, we will let you know just as soon as we find out, so you will have time to look into the matter and shall not be prejudiced by any action upon our part.

We do not know of anything further as that part of our motion for a new trial.

Very respectfully,
W.H. Van Skaik
R.M. Nevin
Attorneys for Defendant

As the motion for a new trial came up before Judge Brown on January 18, 1897, a large crowd once again gathered outside the courthouse. The room inside the courtroom for spectators filled up quickly, and the rest spilled out of the courtroom and into the corridors.

Albert resumed his pale countenance and nervous demeanor in court and placed his head in his hand and elbow on the table. His sister Mattie and a friend exchanged a few words of greeting with Albert before the proceedings began.

The first to testify was J.W. Sortman. Around the time of the second postmortem exam of the body, in the presence of jury foreman George Davis, Sortman commented to another that he believed Albert shot Bessie. Davis agreed with his statement.

Three witnesses, George Gallagher, George Mannix and Clinton Herby, were all called to testify but had nothing with any bearing on this case to say.

James Herby said he had a conversation with juror Joseph Daugherty around the time the blood spots were found on the bridge, in which Daugherty stated he believed Albert committed the crime. According to Herby, Daugherty said he'd had a conversation with Charles Eby, a relative of Albert, and made the same statement to Eby.

David Oliver and his son Alexander, both residents of Poasttown and neighbors to juror Joseph Shively, were asked if they ever heard Shively comment his opinion on the Frantz case. Both stated they never did.

At the conclusion of the motion, Judge Brown emerged from his chambers and read a long statement to the court, stating he was dismissing the motion for a new trial. At the conclusion of his statement, he ordered Albert to stand before him to receive his sentence. Judge Brown asked Albert if he had anything to say before hearing his sentence, and Albert shook his head no. Judge Brown then read his sentence:

> *Albert J. Frantz,*
>
> *You have been accused by the Grand Jury of your country on their oath, with having unlawfully, purposefully, and of deliberate and premeditated malice, murdered Bessie Little by shooting her in the head with a pistol. Upon this accusation you have been put upon trial before a jury of your fellow citizens, almost selected by yourself. They have on their oaths found you guilty of murder in the first degree as you stood charged in the indictment.*
>
> *I now ask you whether you have anything to say why judgment should not be pronounced against you. It now becomes my duty as judge of this court to pronounce the judgment the law has provided for your crime. It is that you be taken hence by the sheriff of this county to the jail of this county, and that within the next thirty days from this date, in as private and secure a manner as possible, you be conveyed by the sheriff to the Ohio Penitentiary at Columbus, Ohio, and by him turned over to the custody of the warden of the said penitentiary and within the walls of said penitentiary, said warden, or, in case of his death, inability or absence, a deputy warden shall, on the 13th day of May in the year eighteen hundred and ninety-seven, and before the hour of sunrise on said day, according to law execute this death sentence, by causing to pass through your body a current of electricity of sufficient intensity to cause death, and the application of such current to be continued until you are dead.*

The execution date of May 13 caused a stir among those superstitiously afraid of the number thirteen. A newspaper article listed several coincidences involving the number thirteen related to the case. There are thirteen letters in "Albert J. Frantz," "Bessie R. Little," "John W. Kreitzer" and "horse and buggy." Albert was thirteen when his mother died on the thirteenth day of the month. His trial was thirteen days long, and the word for his method of execution, *electrocution*, is thirteen letters long.

Shortly after the hearing, Sheriff Anderton carried out Judge Brown's instructions to convey Albert to the Ohio Penitentiary "in as private and secure a manner as possible" within thirty days. Albert's family and attorneys were not notified until after Albert had arrived at the penitentiary.

Albert himself didn't know he was going until Jailor Wood notified him he was about to leave. Jailor Wood himself had less than an hour's notice. Once notified, Albert calmly put on his best clothes and waited. The party escorting Albert consisted of Sheriff Anderton, driver John Smith, court bailiff Boes and jailer Wood, who was handcuffed to Albert for the trip. Nobody noticed as the party left the jail, and they arrived at the depot right on time for the train. From Dayton to Columbus, Albert stared silently out the window, sometimes crying. He was received by warden Coffin in Columbus and taken to the annex, a section of the building dedicated to housing convicted murderers.

There were three other prisoners occupying the annex when Albert arrived. There was William Haas, convicted of the rape and murder of his employer's wife; Frank Miller, also convicted of raping and murdering his employer's wife; and William Wiley, convicted of murdering his wife. Albert kept his spirits up, enjoying the companionship of the other inmates. When together, they were able to forget where they were and simply enjoy time together. On April 21, 1897, William Haas became the first Ohio prisoner to be executed by electrocution, and William Wiley followed later the same day, becoming the second. After the loss of his companions, Albert's mood plummeted.

As the appeal process continued, a stay of execution was granted to allow time for the case to be heard in the circuit court before Judge Summers. Once Judge Summers heard the appeal, he dismissed the case and upheld Judge Brown's decision to deny Albert a second trial. The delivery of the decision took an hour. Judge Summers addressed each claim of error, and in each case, the lower court's decision was sustained. He concluded:

> *There is conflicting testimony as to the claim that jurors Daugherty, Davis, and Von Engle expressed a prior opinion as to Frantz's guilt, but it is held that nothing was said prejudicial to Frantz's interests. In the absence of Frantz's revolver the production for inspection by the jury was admissible in law. The evidence and testimony went to prove either that Bessie Little committed suicide in Albert Frantz's buggy by firing two bullets into her right ear or that Frantz himself killed her by so doing. The burden of the proof went to show the latter as the cause.*

Albert's new execution date was set for October 15, 1897, before sunrise. After losing the appeal in Ohio's supreme court, Albert's attorney's sent a letter to Ohio governor Bushnell, hoping for a pardon. While Bushnell considered the matter, Albert's execution date was delayed again, to November 19, 1897.

It was during the appeal process that two new letters written by Bessie were discovered. Mrs. Freese was cleaning Bessie's old room when she found two letters hidden behind sandpaper tacked to the wall. When Mrs. Freese tore away the sandpaper, the letters were revealed. They were addressed to "Dear Friends at Home" and to "Mrs. Lizzie J. Little, 1638 West Second Street, city."

In the first letter, dated August 13, 1896, Bessie recounted her troubles,

> *While we were out riding I discovered that he carried a revolver. Once he sighed and did not answer when I talked to him. He only put his arm around my neck and said "I will be so glad when we get together for good." He was driving with same hand; put his hand on revolver, and oh! If he would only have fulfilled his purpose! But his courage failed him. He may yet accomplish it. I will be calm when it comes, as I don't care to live. He has broken my heart and ruined my character. I was in Frantz's barn two nights last week. Bert brought a razor, laid it on my neck twice. Oh! How badly he wanted to take my life!*
>
> *Twice now, and also last Saturday night, he made me take all my things from hotel and go out in Riverdale. Said you folks wanted to talk to us, and me to come home; went out where there was not a bit of light; wanted to go down to the bridge over Mad River (probably meant Stillwater Bridge). I guess he would have thrown me over so no one could have found me. I expect to be killed any time by his own hand or someone he employs, for he just hates me.*

Bessie admitted she had taken poison the previous Sunday and it had made her deathly sick. She confessed she was in a delicate condition (or so she thought). She wrote of a recent night in which she went buggy riding with Albert and he had a loaded revolver on the seat between them. Throughout the night, he kept touching the revolver, but it seemed as if his courage "failed him," as Bessie described it.

The second letter was dated August 24, 1896, and was a "recital of her wrongs, but does not tell of any threats," according to the *Cincinnati Enquirer*. Bessie reiterated that Albert had promised to marry her but still hadn't followed through. She closed the letter with: "I am going to take your advice in regard to taking my life, as I suppose that would make him too happy."

Albert's defense attorneys wanted to use these letters as an avenue for a retrial in Albert's case, believing they proved Bessie was suicidal. The state's attorneys denied the importance of the letters. Governor Bushnell said he'd take the matter under consideration along with the other documents submitted. He promised to "do his duty" when it came time.

As the time neared, Albert grew more desolate. As the sun made its decline on November 17, Albert's anxiety prevented him from eating dinner. He wouldn't speak to anyone and simply sat with his hands folded. He went to bed early but scarcely slept all night.

On the morning of November 18, 1897, Albert woke up with a feeling of dread. He still hadn't heard back from Governor Bushnell, and the time of his execution was nearing. Breakfast was broiled tenderloin steak, a ham omelet, French-fried potatoes, toast and butter, coffee, milk and cream. Albert skipped eating but sipped a half cup of coffee. He paced the floor until he was so weak he needed to lie down, then asked for paper and spent the next few hours writing letters. He spent extra time on a letter to a Mr. Anderson of London, Ohio. Tears poured down his cheeks as he wrote, wetting the paper.

After a talk with warden Coffin, Albert perked up a bit. Albert confided in Coffin, still declaring his innocence in the crime. He said despite the fact that witnesses perjured themselves on the stand to convict him, he would not exchange places with any of them. He asked the warden to keep away anyone who assisted in his prosecution, especially the witness who swore to his purchase of the revolver. Dinner consisted of short ribs of beef, brown gravy, braised ox tongue, corn fritters, tomato sauce, mashed potatoes, sliced onions, green gage plum pie, Neapolitan cake, "salines a la ham," coffee and cream. Despite the feast, Albert again refused to eat.

When the telegram finally came from Governor Bushnell, it said:

> *Careful review of the Albert Frantz case does not furnish sufficient reason to my mind to justify executive interference in the execution of the sentence of the court, and the application for commutation is rejected.*
> —*Asa S. Bushnell*

Warden Coffin took the notice to Albert along with his death warrant. He read both documents aloud to Albert in the presence of his family. In attendance were three of his siblings—Mattie, Cornelius and Reverend Isaac—and his cousin Mrs. Teeter. Albert and his family remained silent as warden Coffin read, with the occasional sob escaping from Mattie. When

Coffin was finished, he left the cell. As he walked away, Mattie threw herself onto her brother, embracing him as she cried out, "Oh my poor brother!" Isaac paced the small cell, repeating, "My God, why may not this sorrow pass from us?"

Once Mattie regained her composure, Albert was removed to get a final shave and cut from the prison barber. The barber, Harvey Miller, was serving a seventeen-year sentence for manslaughter. Coincidentally, Harvey Miller was a boyhood friend of Albert's from Montgomery County.

Albert and his family were allowed to share his last meal. Albert sat between his brothers, Isaac and Cornelius. Mattie sat across from Albert. As a Dunkard minister, Reverend Isaac offered a long prayer before eating.

After dinner, Albert divided his last items among his family. To Mattie, he gave his pocketbook. To Mrs. Teeter, a ring. He divided his watch charm and other personal items between the remaining brothers. Together, Albert's family sang "Rock of Ages, Cleft for Me," and Isaac offered up an earnest prayer for his baby brother.

When it came time to part ways, Mattie lost control, gripping Albert and kissing him goodbye. Her sobs could be heard throughout the corridor. Isaac and Cornelius broke down too. With great difficulty, the guard broke the family members and Albert apart and escorted his family from the annex. The procession of the family through the corridor to their carriage affected even the most hardened criminals in the annex. They uncovered and bowed their heads in respect as the family walked past. Mrs. Coffin, the warden's wife, and their daughter escorted the family in an attempt to provide comfort.

Breaking his stoic persona, Albert was overcome with emotion. As warden Coffin separated Albert from his sister's embrace, Albert fell to the floor. Chaplain Winget and guard Bowman had to help him to his bed and allow him to rest before he was restored to complete consciousness.

Chapter 15

EXECUTION

November 19, 1897

A crowd of hundreds showed up in hopes of obtaining admission to the execution. The guardroom was packed with eager men, many inebriated and all noisy. Multiple times, "Big John" Langenberger, captain of the night watch, cleared the guardroom, just to have it filled up again within minutes. It took several attempts and gentle force to get the mob of interested onlookers away from the door.

When he finally started admitting members of the crowd, Langenberger called first for physicians. Most applicants who responded were not physicians and were turned away. Next called for were reporters, and again, many who never wrote a word responded to the call and were turned away. When, finally, more onlookers were allowed, the execution room filled well past capacity. In all, 175 people were admitted to a room normally limited to 75 to view the electrocution, and several hundred more packed into the corridors and spilled onto the lawn of the state prison. Chairs had long been filled before the start of the execution, and the rest of the crowd stood and sat in the remaining space on the floor. Only those seated very close to the execution chair could actually see anything. The crowd buzzed with excitement, talking and laughing as if attending a party rather than an execution. The rowdiness reached its peak when a law student from Dayton attempted to strike another man in the room. He was ejected and returned later but was forced to the back of the room by the crowd. Officials enforced order and silence before Albert walked into the room.

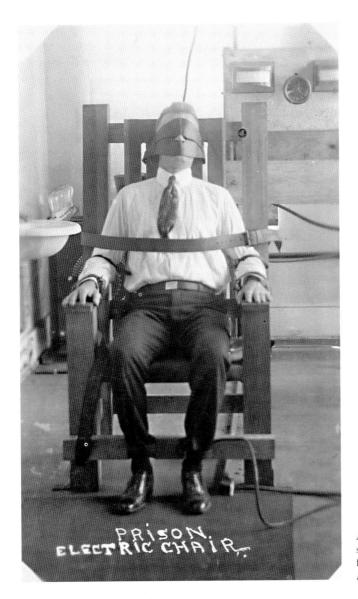

PRISON.
ELECTRIC CHAIR.

An electric chair,
similar to the one used
for Albert's execution.
Public domain.

At seventeen minutes past midnight, Albert entered the execution room, led by Chaplain Winget, who had been praying with him. All color had drained from his face. Despite his circumstances, he was calm and collected, as if he were simply taking a walk. He walked straight to the chair and sat in it, turning to a guard, Bowman, and saying goodbye.

As Albert was secured in the chair with straps, men elbowed each other in attempts to silence the crowd for the spectacle about to take place.

Guard Bowman continued the process of strapping Albert into the chair. Heavy leather bands were secured across his chest and abdomen and over his wrists, ankles, knees and elbows. The electrical expert placed a band across Albert's forehead, and appliances were attached to the band to keep a sponge in place.

When the last buckles were secured, Albert told warden Coffin, "Warden, I am prepared to die, I have made my peace with God."

The time was called out, and a black mask was pulled over Albert's face. A dampened sponge was placed atop his head. His thick hair had been premoistened with sal ammoniac (ammonium chloride) in the spot where the sponge was to go, but in the haste of preparation, the sponge was placed in the wrong spot, on a dry part of his hair. A tense quiet hung in the air as the warden stood next to the lever, awaiting the signal. After several long moments, the switch was flipped. A cloud of blue smoke filled the room, and the sickening smell of burning hair permeated the air. Albert's body sprang against the straps and then sank back into the chair, uttering a loud groan when the current was turned off. Physicians went to his side to check for signs of life. After several moments, Dr. Farrell, who was assisting the prison physicians, announced loudly so the crowd could hear, "His heart is still beating."

The straps that had been loosened to allow the physicians to examine Albert were tightened again. On went the current, and Albert's body flailed against the straps, releasing more burnt-hair stench into the air. A groan emanated from his body as his chest contracted and he attempted to draw in breath. His pulse was still present, so a third attempt was made. In total, it took five attempts of 1,700 volts. At 12:25 a.m., Albert was pronounced dead.

Once death was pronounced, Albert's body was removed from the chair, laid out on the floor and covered with a blue checkered piece of cloth usually used to cover the chair. The room was cleared, and undertaker Isaac Funderburg, of Funderburg & Helvie in New Carlisle, was given charge of Albert's remains. Isaac Funderburg was chosen at the request of the Frantz family since he was Albert's cousin. The family requested no postmortem exam, although it was customary following an execution. Albert's remains were shipped to New Carlisle to be buried in the family plot.

Albert's funeral was a small, private affair, held at undertaker Funderburg's place. The hearse was led by two matching white horses. Funderburg sat in the hearse wearing a frock coat, a tall silk hat and white gloves. There was no service, but Reverend W.I. Hoover spoke briefly beside Albert's grave at Studebaker Cemetery. Only two of Albert's friends were present to be pallbearers, so the undertaker's sons made up the other four. Albert's remains were encased in a steel receptacle to prevent tampering with his body, and he was interred next to his mother. A large crowd gathered at the cemetery but were not admitted. Although many had no feeling left for Albert, they felt sympathy for his relatives, especially his father. Many were concerned that the stress of the trial, the shock of the execution and the loss of his son would be too much for him.

Bessie was disinterred one last time, to reunite head and body. She was finally given a Christian burial and laid to rest in Woodland Cemetery. The service, attended by a few of Bessie's friends and her "parents," was conducted by Reverend Gigsby, her former pastor.

The revolver for which Chief Farrell spent many hours searching was "found" three times in the years after Bessie's death. In September 1905, a revolver was found by two farm hands clearing the woods near the bridge. Two chambers were empty, and it was very rusty. Two years later, in August 1907, Samuel Hale was fishing in the Stillwater River when he found a rusty revolver in the water. In May 1917, yet another rusty revolver was found in the riverbed one hundred feet north of the bridge. Each of these revolvers was suspected, but never proven, to be the one used to kill Bessie Little.

Over one hundred years have passed, and the "Bessie Little Bridge" is more commonly known today as the Ridge Avenue Bridge. Stories of Bessie's ghost have become far less common over time, but every once in a while, some claim to have seen her standing on the bridge, staring into the water. Sometimes when the air is still and the night is quiet, you can hear a scream followed by two shots, then a splash. If you listen closely enough, perhaps you may hear lines from a song written after Albert's death:

Just tell them that I shot her
She never knew it was done
Just tell them she was looking
Sweet, you know.
She whispered as she breathed her last,
"Dear Bert, what have you done?"

BIBLIOGRAPHY

Buckeye (Troy, OH). "Albert J. Frantz." November 25, 1897.
Buffalo Evening News. "Weaving a Gallows Loop." December 29, 1896.
Cincinnati Enquirer. "Battery of Powerful Magnets." September 8, 1896.
———. "Flesh of Frantz Burned." November 19, 1897.
———. "Letters." November 11, 1897.
———. "Like an Avenging Specter Appeared the Head of Bessie Little." December 18, 1896.
———. "Mystery Both Dark and Deep." September 4, 1896.
———. "Seen by a Man and Woman." December 30, 1896.
———. "Stopped." December 30, 1896.
Cincinnati Post. "Death Is a Penalty Frantz Must Pay." June 21, 1897.
Columbus Republican. "Albert Frantz Electrocuted." November 25, 1897.
Daily Democrat (Huntington, Indiana). "Made a Confession." September 11, 1896.
Dayton Daily News. "Revolver Which May Have Caused Death of Bessie Little Is Found." May 27, 1917.
Dayton Herald. "Albert Frantz." January 26, 1897.
———. "Albert J. Frantz." April 24, 1897.
———. "A New Trial." December 31, 1896.
———. "Another 'Bessie Little Gun' Found." August 29, 1907.
———. "Bessie Little's Head." December 17, 1896.
———. "The Death Penalty." November 19, 1897.
———. "The Doctors." September 9, 1896.

———. "Frantz Case." January 13, 1897.

———. "Frantz Confesses." September 10, 1896.

———. "Frantz Spends a Quiet Christmas in Jail." December 25, 1896.

———. "Frantz's Revolver." December 18, 1896.

———. "The Grave Closes." November 22, 1897.

———. "Has Broken Down." November 18, 1897.

———. "He Must Die." January 23, 1897.

———. "Hinted at Suicide." December 23, 1896.

———. "It Was Murder." September 7, 1896.

———. "The Last Appeal." November 16, 1897.

———. "The Motion." January 18, 1897.

———. "No Action Taken." November 17, 1897.

———. "Prosecution Rests." December 22, 1896.

———. "Really Pitiful." December 25, 1896.

———. "Revolver, Believed Used in Murdering Young Woman, Found." May 28, 1907.

———. "The Search." September 11, 1896.

———. "Startling Developments in the Bessie Little Case." September 5, 1896.

———. "Suicide or Murder?" September 3, 1896.

———. "That Fatal Night." December 21, 1896.

———. "Was She Murdered?" September 4, 1896.

———. "A Wild Scene." December 30, 1896.

———. "With Magnets." September 8, 1896.

———. "Without Bond." September 15, 1896.

———. "A Woman's Screams." December 19, 1896.

Delphos Daily Herald. "Frantz's Confession." September 12, 1896.

Evening Bulletin (Maysville, KY). "Bessie Little Buried." December 13, 1897.

Indianapolis Journal. "Bessie Little's Murder." September 12, 1896.

Kentucky Post and Times-Star. "Devil's Deed." September 7, 1896.

———. "Head." December 17, 1896.

———. "His Fate." December 19, 1896.

———. "His Sister." December 24, 1896.

———. "Is It Murder?" September 5, 1896.

———. "Judge Brown to the Jury." December 29, 1896.

———. "Located." September 12, 1896.

———. "Mollie Cart." December 22, 1896.

———. "A Mysterious Bundle." September 9, 1896.

———. "One Link." September 5, 1896.

———. "Satisfied." September 11, 1896.

———. "Waiting." December 25, 1896.

———. "Weighing the Bullets." December 18, 1896.

Kentucky Post. "His Love for Another." September 10, 1896.

———. "In Tears." December 23, 1896.

———. "Professor Stone's Study of Albert Frantz." December 21, 1897.

Kentucky Times-Star. "River's Dark Secret." September 8, 1896.

Lima Clipper. "Killed by Her Lover." September 18, 1896.

Lima News. "Slayer's Revolver Is Found." September 26, 1905.

Philadelphia Enquirer. "A Bullet in Her Head." September 6, 1896.

San Francisco Examiner. "The Mysterious Murder of Bessie Little." October 4, 1896.

St. Louis Globe. "Albert Frantz Electrocuted." November 19, 1897.

Taylor, W.J. "Pistol." *Cincinnati Enquirer.* December 28, 1896.

———. "Play." *Cincinnati Enquirer.* December 29, 1896.

Wilkes-Barre Record. "Frantz Electrocuted." November 20, 1897.

Xenia Daily Gazette. "Bessie Little." November 11, 1897.

———. "Dr. Bonner in the Bessie Little Case." January 6, 1897.

———. "Fatal Thirteen." January 27, 1897.

———. "The Frantz Trial." December 18, 1896.

———. "Saw the Murder." December 31, 1896.

———. "Testimony All In." December 26, 1896.

Young, Roz. "Poor Albert Frantz." *Dayton Daily News.* October 6, 1990.

ABOUT THE AUTHOR

Sara Kaushal is a Dayton historian, the author of *Murder & Mayhem in Dayton and the Miami Valley* and *Dayton Ghosts & Legends* and the primary author of the blog *Dayton Unknown*. She loves historic true crime, mysteries and ghost stories and can't drive through Dayton without pointing out at least one haunted place. She has a bookshelf full of books she intends to read one day, when she's not researching or writing. Sara can be contacted for events and questions at authorsarakaushal@gmail.com.